By the same author

Getting Better All the Time

Ruffles and Flourishes

Unplanned
Parenthood

Unplanned Parenthood

*The Confessions of
a Seventysomething
Surrogate Mother*

Liz Carpenter

Random House New York

All rights reserved under International and Pan-American
Copyright Conventions. Published in the United States by
Random House, Inc., New York, and simultaneously in Canada
by Random House of Canada Limited, Toronto.

Library of Congress Cataloging-in-Publication Data
Carpenter, Liz.
Unplanned parenthood : the confessions of a
seventy-something surrogate mother / Liz Carpenter.—1st ed.
p. cm.
ISBN 0-679-42798-8
1. Carpenter, Liz. 2. Foster parents—Texas—Biography.
3. Aunts—Texas—Biography.
4. Journalists—Texas—Biography.
5. Parent and teenager—Texas—Case studies. I. Title.
HQ759.7.C37 1994
362.7′33′092—dc20   94-13995
[B]

Manufactured in the United States of America
24689753
First Edition

To my late brother,

Tom,

who made this experience possible

Sometimes you don't have no control over the way things go. Hail ruins the crops or fire burns you out.

And then you're just given so much to work with in a life and you have to do the best you can with what you've got.

That's what piecing is.

The materials is passed on to you or is all you can afford to buy . . . your fate.

But the way you put them together is your business.

You can put them in any order you like.

MARY WHITE, *The Quilters*

What is this I hear of sorrow and weariness,
Anger, discontent, and drooping hopes?
Degenerate sons and daughters,
Life is too strong for you.
It takes life to love Life.

LUCINDA MATLOCK, *Spoon River Anthology*

Acknowledgments

A thousand thanks to . . .

—My literary agent, Doe Coover, who—when I was telling her about a book I was writing on friendship—said, "How are you getting along with raising the kids?" I told her—for an hour—antics and heartbreaks, and she said, "Forget about friendship. You and the kids are the book."

—My distinguished and affable editor, Bob Loomis, who believed it too.

—President and Mrs. Clinton, who asked us all to dinner at the White House.

—Lady Bird Johnson, who said, "Ya'll come on over for supper" time after time.

—Her daughters, Lynda Robb and Luci Johnson,

who went through their children's closets each season and sent boxes of hand-me-downs.

—Her niece, Patsy Chaney, who brought her famous Presbyterian Chicken and Rice Casserole countless times.

—My beloved brother and sister-in-law, George and Jean Sutherland, who were always there with unconditional love when I needed them.

—Soul mates like Harry Middleton, who was willing to read every word of this book and be frank about the bad and the good, and Marshall De Bruhl, whose dim view of child-rearing gave me some of the best lines.

—Friends who know a lot more about teenagers than I did: Anita Davis, Sue Drake, Shirley James, Jacque Goettsche.

—Those who kept me going with tender loving care and medical advice, day or night: Dr. Billy Bailey, Mary Love Bailey, Dr. Don Baxter, and Dr. Mary Maxwell.

—Good friends who were willing to read and critique: Betty Sue Flowers and Cynthia Maddox.

—The G-Bats, my singing group, who let me be late or absent from rehearsals and kept me on key in so many ways.

—My own two children, Scott and Christy, who could have told me not to do it, but didn't.

—Nancy Nelson Sutherland, the children's

mother, who read it, liked it, and laughed out loud on cue.

—And, of course, Paula Stout, who was my memory, my legs, my confidante, and ever helpful and happy-hearted from the first word of this book to the last.

—And finally, the kids themselves—Mary, Tommy, and Liz—who were, well, teenagers, that age group that drives you to mayhem or mother-love. Without them, there would have been no book, no adventure, no opening of horizons I never knew existed.

Contents

Contents

Foreword

*I*n September of 1991, I arrived in San Antonio, Texas, to receive an award from the Southwest Society on Aging for "exploding myths about aging and older people."

I was sure it was a case of mistaken identity, as I was in deep denial about being sixty-four. I insisted editors run my high-school graduation picture over my column, and if Willard Scott ever called to wish me happy birthday I was going to report him to the phone company for obscenity.

Liz Carpenter had received the award the year before and had agreed to introduce me. She was running late. This wasn't like Liz. Less than an hour before the luncheon, she came to my room and announced she had just come from her brother's funeral. Then she added, "Would you think I was crazy if I agreed to raise his two teenagers and his twelve-year-old?"

"If you are looking for adventure," I said, "why don't you go to Mt. Rushmore, attach a bungee cord to Lincoln's wart, and jump!"

I knew *why* she was considering it. Because Liz couldn't bear to stand by and see three children struggling with life—alone. I just didn't know *how* she was going to do it.

Liz Carpenter always made Auntie Mame look like a shut-in. We traveled together for several years around the country trying to get the ERA passed into law. We did this by giving the razorback hog call in Arkansas, dining with heads of the teamsters unions, and auctioning off my husband's underwear. In between appearances we talked into the small hours of the morning. She wanted me to call the pope to ask him to trade abortion for the ERA.

Liz lectured, wrote books and columns, partied, and belonged to the Bay at the Moon Society, who would sing at the drop of a pitch pipe.

On her infamous vacation trips, she was like a rocket in flight. One night in Mexico we were en route to a party in a cab, and Liz, in an effort to prove that three people could fit in the front seat, had to straddle the gearshift in the floor. She conceded, "Every time the driver put the taxi in first gear, it was a religious experience."

Her friends all wondered if a woman entering her seventies could make the transition to brownies and curfews. Could she absorb all the changes since she raised her own children thirty years ago? Or would she drop the kids off and forget where she left them? The only thing I could see in her favor was that she had a hearing problem, and their music could sound like a helicopter hovering over the house and she wouldn't hear it.

On the other hand, I couldn't help but envy these three children. They would occupy a house with a woman who gives special meaning to "seize the day." She not only seizes it, she grabs it by the throat and shakes it until there is nothing left of it. While other people talk a dream to death—Liz makes it happen. Her zest for living is contagious. She would peel off the layers of life for these children and let them taste it all like an exotic fruit.

If they allowed her, she would share with them her wisdom, her enthusiasm, her Rolodex of friends that sounds like a Who's Who in America, her values, and her decency.

Those of us who have raised teenagers know "it's not a good time" to speak or travel with them, ask questions, or discipline them. They all have an orphan wish that doesn't dissipate until they need money for their first car.

By her own description she is a woman with "one

bosom gone, one deaf ear, a swollen arthritic ankle, and the weakest bladder in Travis County." Could she pull it off? The rules of child raising had all changed. Ask any grandmother who has had to assume the mother role. Today's children speak a different language, have different expectations and their own moral code. It is still a full-time job and a lifetime commitment.

Liz has put it all down in this book. But what sparkles in her chronicles of a biological clock that refuses to die is her humor. Those of us (including myself) who were skeptical may have missed something about Liz Carpenter. Something important. Maybe her curiosity and zest for life have been fueled by challenges and new mountains to climb. She is a unique human being because she is continually writing new chapters in her life. I hope she publishes them all.

—ERMA BOMBECK

Unplanned Parenthood

1

My Brother's Keeper

*F*irst off, you should know I was bitten by a mad dog when I was six. So right off I got used to unexpected events in my life.

At the time, the summer of 1926, I was at my grandmother's house in the country and my four-year-old brother, George, and I were out in the front yard playing in a persimmon grove when the dog got us both.

For months the newspapers in Texas had been filled with stories of what happened to people bitten by rabid dogs if they did not head immediately for the Pasteur Institute at the Texas State Insane Asylum in Austin and get twenty-one shots in the stomach. We were warned we would foam at the mouth, start biting people, and ultimately die in a fit.

My Uncle Maclin put the dog in a cage and drove

him sixty miles to Austin, where the Institute found the rabies. After my uncle raced back to us in Salado with the sobering news, my mother packed our clothes and away we went in a Model T Ford to take my longest trip up to that point in my life. Mama rented rooms in a boardinghouse, and for twenty-one days she walked us across the street each morning to wait our turn for the shots, took us to the nearby drugstore for the promised ice cream cone, and then boarded us on the streetcar to see the sights in the largest and most interesting town we had ever been in.

The experience of the dog bite affected George and me in different ways. George became a rabid Republican and I became a rabid Democrat. I still swear the dog was "yaller" and George claims it was white— lily-pure white.

Surprisingly, the whole event turned out to be completely happy except for the dog and the daily shot, and from it I learned early in life that what looks like a disaster can lead to a widening world. Which brings me to what I'm doing right now: raising my brother's three kids—teenagers to boot—at the age of seventy-four as I move from what I always assumed would be a permanent state of madcap youth into what I suspect is a slightly dotty old age.

So you'll know where I'm coming from, let me take time to tell you. I don't have any complaints about

life. It's been good to me, better than I ever anticipated. Of course, there are a few things here and
there I would change. I wish my education had been
classical enough for me to give a damn about Aristotle, and I certainly wish I still had my husband,
who died at fifty-three, just when our children were
out of college. We could have had more golden
times and he would have relished our children's
success and our grandchildren. And I wish President
Kennedy hadn't been killed that dreadful November
day when we were motorcading through Dallas.

It was a day that changed my life as well as everyone else's in the country. Through the shock and the
sorrow that followed I found myself a White House
player, working alongside Lyndon and Lady Bird
Johnson as LBJ successfully pushed forward many
of the New Frontier programs that had been log-
jammed in Congress, and then won passage for his
own dramatic initiations like the Voting Rights Act
and the unprecedented drive for educational assis-
tance, embodied in more than a hundred bills. I
doubt if anyone else could have enacted as much
legislation for the people.

As a young Washington reporter, I had covered
LBJ during the 1940s and 1950s when he was a
congressman, then senator, and ultimately vice
president–elect in 1960. That's when he asked me to
come down from the press galleries and "share the

great adventure of our lives." It was exhilarating to work for him and for Lady Bird while he was vice president, and then during their five years in the White House. It opened my eyes to our country's needs and gave me a chance to help. It *was* a great adventure.

By heritage and by profession, I am a storyteller. Like all good Southerners I can spin a yarn on any occasion with only a hint of an invitation. I have been writing and talking for my living since I was twenty-two and first went to Washington. So telling this story of a septuagenarian taking in three sad and confused teenagers to raise is in that garrulous tradition.

The experience of bringing these children under my roof and aging wing has been fabulous and funny and painful. It began with my liking them and resulted in my loving them. *Most days.* Had I been an artist, I might have tried to capture them on a canvas. Had I been a songwriter, they could have inspired a ballad. But I am a writer, so I have to do it my way.

Three years have passed since they came home with me. At first it was just Mary and Tommy, the two youngest of my brother's offspring, so blond and too shy to talk except when I asked them a question. Liz, my namesake, the oldest of his second family, is darker in eyes and hair. She followed a few months later to finish high school with me because she couldn't bear being separated from her younger siblings.

Fortunately I had grown up in an elastic, loving, extended family where everyone was welcome to stay for dinner or for four years of university time. My mother was like that. We had moved from the small town of Salado down the road sixty miles to Austin so she could put us through the University of Texas, which beckoned ranch and farm children from Muleshoe to Cut and Shoot, Texas, to "come and get educated."

My mother believed that if the sleeping porch had room, and you had the $12.50 enrollment fee for the university, then come on and join us. Several cousins got their education that way. That was before the social arbiters began advising us to clear the house of grandmothers, maiden aunts, and anyone else who could help and might have an influence on the children that would burden them with stress. Stress has had a bum rap. I think it beats boredom hands down.

The ordered world of those long-ago childhood and college days, when everyone knew what the Golden Rule was whether they observed it or not, began to change, as did the fabric of life itself, under the pressures of World War II.

By 1942 I had gone to Washington, D.C., with my journalism degree in hand and my virtue intact. (I still have my journalism degree.) In 1944 I had married my college sweetheart, Leslie Carpenter, who was a journalist too. And when he was through serving as a lieutenant (j.g.) in the Navy, we established a news bureau in that great city of politics and intrigue. The years in Washington were full of adventure and excitement. I was there in time to cover a few of FDR's last press conferences. This was when reporters still worked with ancient writing tools like pads and pencils, with only a microphone or two for radio, mind you. So about seventy-five of us would stand around the Oval Office as Roosevelt sat relaxed behind his desk, cigarette holder at a jaunty tilt, jousting with the press. Today's press conferences are like a Texas cattle auction, where the loudest and pushiest reporter gets the beef . . . or the bull. I should have seen it coming when all the men in Washington started wearing light blue shirts and maroon ties because they photographed better on the evening news. We women, in turn, shucked our hats and gloves and trimmed down to fighting weight to join the fracas.

Through the fifties I was spellbound watching the great theater of Congress. Les and I hung over the press galleries of the House and Senate to see Madame Chiang Kai-shek, in her slim embroidered satin dress with the split skirt, plead for money to arm her general's army, now pushed out of China to Taiwan.

We were at the press table in the House Caucus Room to observe the confrontation between Alger Hiss and Whittaker Chambers, the man whose "pumpkin papers" were the making of Richard Nixon.

In the crowded press gallery I listened to General MacArthur, who had been fired for insubordination by an indignant Harry Truman, deliver his memorable exit speech about old soldiers fading away. To the cheers of the chamber, he strode down the aisle, pausing halfway to salute his wife in the gallery. America loved it. But my cynical seatmate, who knew theater when he saw it, muttered: "Next week, Hamlet."

"Yes," I replied. "We've already had the ham."

Washington remained a magical assignment even as the rhythm changed from the frenetic pace of the Truman years to the sonorous drifting of the Eisenhower era. And then the excitement of the Kennedy time, when I turned in my reporter's badge for a staff assignment with Vice President Lyndon Johnson. I was there that day in Dallas, and riding numb with shock across the city to board *Air Force One* with the new president and first lady, I penciled the fifty-eight words that Johnson spoke when we arrived at An-

drews Air Force base: "This is a sad time for all people. We have suffered a loss that cannot be weighed.
For me, it is a deep personal tragedy. I know that the
world shares the sorrow that Mrs. Kennedy and her
family bear. I will do my best. That is all I can do. I
ask for your help—and God's."

When the Johnsons moved into the White House,
I picked my new job: press secretary and staff director to the first lady.

We seemed so young, Les and I, flush with energy
and dreams of raising our new family enveloped in
the power, glory, and heart of our country. Someone
called it "the springtime of our lives," heady stuff
mixed with hard work, tears, and laughter, the iro-
nies and mischief-making of politics. And along with
it all the raising of our own two children, Scott and
Christy. Our daily lives were crowded with the sweep
of larger events that absorbed these Texas reporters.
The ever-breaking news stories were our work and
our lives.

After LBJ left the presidency, a day that will live in
infamy, in our household at least, I went home, sat
down, and wrote about my five White House years of
answering questions instead of asking them. *Ruffles
and Flourishes* was published in 1969 and soon after
I went to work at Hill and Knowlton Public Relations
as the vice president in charge of Democrats.

For thirty-four marvelous years Les and I had lived

fully. But then in 1974 Les died and life changed. My children were grown and pursuing their own careers: they were financially and emotionally independent. Of course, they were there for me if I needed them. But my household had shrunk from four to one. Luckily I was rich with friends, many of them big names in the news then and later to be the headline makers. Still, Washington didn't feel right. Something vital was missing. And that something was Les, who had always made me feel cherished, who needed me as I needed him. Washington had been our town when we were together, but I kept feeling it wasn't "my" town anymore. Les was gone, the Republicans were in charge, and life was stale and empty. Maybe I had tasted the best and should move on.

Three things prodded me back to Texas. One was the fact that widowhood had given me that widow-look. You know what I mean. It's unmistakable. Not quite stockings rolled down to the ankles and too much rouge, but close. I remembered a statue called *Grief,* a tribute to Henry Adams's wife in the Rock Creek Cemetery in D.C. It's a sexless figure—maybe man, maybe woman—dressed in a hooded cloak, the face absolutely emotionless, no sorrow, no joy. Was I to be like this? A longtime friend said, "You've got to come out of that blue funk you're in." I was jarred, but I realized what no one else had the nerve to tell me—I was casting a pall over everyone around me.

And then another friend, an older woman and a recent widow, took both of my hands in hers, looked me in the eye, and said, "Liz, you've got to think of it this way: God has given you a chance at a second life."

So I came home to Texas and for seventeen years savored every day of that second life. I bought a house with a skyline view and a Texas-size outdoor Jacuzzi and filled them both with friends old and new who supplied the laughter and zest that helped me to move from grief into the "happy hours" of my life. I earned my living writing and speaking. To my amazement there were lots of organizations between El Paso and Atlanta that would pay to hear about the local Texas girl who'd been loose in Washington all those years. And as a founding member of the National Women's Political Caucus I went out to preach the gospel of feminism and the need for an equal rights amendment. I was busy again, and happy.

On the day I moved in, I named the house and the acre of land Grassroots, for I was back home in Texas again, which my forebears helped shape when they came by boat and horseback in 1829, before Texas was part of the United States. I settled comfortably into this house of limestone rock, set under seven sheltering oak trees and overlooking the capital city below and beyond. It was and is my "Forever House," where I continued to write about life in general, and mine in particular, content to consign the exciting past to memorabilia on my living-room shelves— mainly pictures of me with most of the eleven presidents and first ladies I have known, a human rights award from the United Nations, a distinguished-alumnae plaque from my university. At first I thought the display might look as if I were bragging, but then someone told me about the Texas woman who was visiting London and showed up at an afternoon party dripping diamonds, rubies, and emeralds.

"My dear," remarked the hostess, "one doesn't wear such jewels in the daytime."

"If you have 'em, you do," replied the Texan.

What excited me about this second life were the times ahead, the excursion into "the last of life, for which the first was made." Even with my calcifying bones I turn resilient at the cocktail hour. My house is not lonely, but a stop for activist friends old and new. Good talk is the *noire faire.*

Then came 1991 and the second great whammy of my declining years: God was offering me a *third* crack at a new life, but this was one I was not at all sure I wanted. My oldest brother and soul mate, Tom, was dying, leaving behind three teenage children who had been raised in haphazard circumstances, the products of his late and careless years. He adored these kids from his second marriage. He and their mother were divorced, but the three children, a boy, fourteen, and two girls, sixteen and almost twelve, lived with their father. He had hoped one of his first family, seven older daughters, would take them on, as they were younger, energetic, and much more with it as far as kids are concerned, but their lives were already full.

There was panic in his eyes and in his husky voice when we talked. He needed to die in peace, and so I assured him I would be there for him, for them. Three weeks before he died, I brought Tommy and Mary, the two youngest, across town to my house on the hill as school opened and Tom's condition worsened. Liz, the oldest, had decided to move in with her mother. It was supposed to be temporary, just until Tom felt better, he said. But I knew different. I knew he wasn't going to feel better. And I also knew once those kids were under my roof, with the cable TV, the cordless phone, and three square meals a day, there'd be no going back. It was very likely the situation would be permanent, and I asked myself the same questions every night: Could I do it? Physically? Mentally? Emotionally? What about financially? Tom had only a small estate, and I knew the high cost of feeding, clothing, and schooling his growing kids (not to mention paying for rock concert tickets and designer shampoo) would fall to me.

My Southern training has taught me never to talk

about money—too crass. But now I would have to face whether I could carry these new members of my family along with my own champagne tastes. Writing and lecturing kept me supported, but they weren't that lucrative.

Why me? Why this unexpected gift to a woman entering her seventies who bore the scars and infirmities of two lifetimes already lived and who had just settled into the promise of a serene but rollicking old age?

Why me?

I was assaulted by indignation that this responsibility was thrust upon me. But the indignation was no match for the overwhelming awareness that these children stared at a future whose door was closed. And that I—aged though I am—seemed to be the only one who could help them push it open.

How little did I know that these years ahead would awaken me to the wider national problem of who is to care for America's children. It would also carry me across the generation gap to learn what the world is like today for them.

It's four P.M. School is out and they're home again. God help me! Well, us. They are engaging kids and I miss them when they're not here, but they are like all teenagers and that means lots of growing-up problems and demands each day.

Liz, who is seventeen, is pulling up in her old blue pickup truck with the classic-rock radio station bumper sticker on it. The truck has seen better days. Make that years! It's sixteen years old but looks ancient with many scars of misuse. I can always tell when she's coming because the truck coughs and sputters its way up the hill, barely making it to the driveway. She'll be rushing in shortly and grabbing the mail to see if any college catalogues have arrived. She's been impatiently awaiting the New York School of Visual Arts summer catalogue. She wants to be a cinematographer. The catalogue is not there and she's going to be disappointed. She'll have to be satisfied with the crossword puzzle and flipping through our sweepstakes magazines until *Jeopardy* comes on.

Down the hill and moving closer I can hear a whirling noise and feel the beat of a stereo. A quick flash of red and car doors slamming announce that Tommy and Mary have arrived in the old second-hand BMW that has more aches than I do.

Tommy, newly sixteen and already six feet tall, is headed for the fridge. He's all arms and legs now, and he attacks food like an octopus, arms flying through the shelves to find the cheese, grab a bagel, swallow a pitcher of milk left over since breakfast, and inhale anything else edible. He just can't get filled up. Look at him now. He's managed to grab a frozen dinner out of the freezer and is setting the microwave. I've learned to hide supper or he'd eat the whole thing before I have a chance to serve it. This isn't my first time with hungry teenagers. Thirty years ago my own son and daughter could go through milkshakes and hamburgers at a pretty good clip, but Tommy beats them cold with his hunger ballet, whirling and twirling around the refrigerator and the microwave with grace that Mikhail Baryshnikov would envy.

Mary, thirteen, has already grabbed the package of peanut butter cookies from the pantry and is in her favorite position for talking on the phone. The blue-flowered couch just fits her and she balances my favorite sofa pillow, emblazoned with a needlepoint slogan that says UPPITY WOMEN UNITE, between her feet for the hour or so she will be talking in a low voice to Kim or Kevin or who knows? I hope it's not long distance. Tommy once set a world's record with a call to Florida for 129 minutes. About sunset, Mary may hang up; then it's television, watching *Night Court* (harmless—at least law and order prevail) or reruns of MTV (not harmless; in my opinion, MTV is sure to make viewers deaf, violent sex maniacs). Mary likes to brush her reddish-blond hair and let it fall over one eye. She's very pretty and can be great and smart, if she survives being thirteen.

The stereo here at home is already on. It is playing R.E.M.'s (which stands for Rapid Eye Movement)

"Man on the Moon" from their latest album, *Automatic for the People.* I learned to recognize the song after the fifteenth time I had heard it. The shortest time span going is between the arrival of these kids and the sound of music, if you can call it music.

I'll see my clean house transformed into a trail of shoes, socks, and book bags—killer book bags. I can't believe the weight of their schoolbooks. Even Arnold Schwarzenegger couldn't lift them without getting a hernia.

There is no getting around it, my job as a stand-in parent gets tougher each day. Maybe, if I keep doing water aerobics and lay off the ice cream, I might live another ten years. I need to live, God.

So there is the answer to "Why me?"

Because there is no one else. And because I would rather do it than fail to do it.

That's why I'm here at the door, fridge overflowing, stereo at the ready, phone on auto-dial (two lines, call-waiting), ready to welcome home my brother's children—now pretty much my own—at four P.M. each day.

2

Four-Star Funeral

$\mathcal{T}$o know who these children are, you need to know something about their father. And the best way I can describe my brother Tom is to tell you about his funeral. It was all-encompassing, a four-star send-off that spoke volumes about Tom Sutherland and his household.

Not many funerals get a newspaper review. A rave review no less! But his did: about five columns across the front page of the City-State section of the *Austin American Statesman*.

When he died, Tom had five saddles in his living room and nineteen Arabian horses just out of town on twenty acres. He also had ten children from two batches: seven middle-aged daughters by his first wife, Lois, and three young teenagers by his second wife, Nancy, who delighted him with the long-awaited son, Thomas Shelton Sutherland the Fifth, called Tommy. The boy was born on April Fool's Day, evidence that God does have a sense of humor. The two daughters by Nancy were named Nancy Elizabeth—Liz (for her mother and me)—and Mary Robertson for our mother. At the time of our mother's death, Tom had written the epitaph for her tombstone: "She was the best evidence of an Almighty Loving Spirit, for nothing else could have created her."

Both ex-wives, Lois and Nancy, had divorced him. Yet both were there at the funeral. In fact, everyone was there, crowded into the back and standing in the door and spilling outside.

The oldest daughters, now in their forties and fifties, arranged the props and planned the service. In front of his pine casket, banked like a Mexican grave, were his favorite keepsakes—a worn cowboy hat, a rope, spurs, a Mexican serape, and a spray of wildflowers and grasses. They knew their father and chose things that were characteristic of him.

He would have loved this funeral service, this affectionate portrait of the Old Texan who spent his life collecting guns, knives, horses, literature, and, yes, children. A strange mix for a university professor of English. But he liked having the artifacts around just to look at, and to show his family and friends. Guns and knives represented life and adventure to him, the American West when it was raw, and preferable to the citification of Texas.

He had picked them up from vagabond days in Mexico and, later, from his fanatical commitment to Saturday morning garage sales. Garage sales were my brother's addiction. When you really got down to it, life—his and other people's—had furnished his home. It was his habit, early on a Saturday morning, to rouse one of his older daughters out of bed by telephone to drive him on the rounds of garage sales. One of them would come, and whoever was awake of the second batch of kids, Tommy, Mary, or Liz, would go along. Everyone has a favorite "garage sale memory." He carried a cup of coffee in hand and, as age set in, leaned on an arm of a child to steady himself. But he always had a cheerful greeting to the people he bartered with.

Columnist Billy Porterfield, who was a literary soul mate and understood Tom and Old Texas, came to the service to write about it. Next day, everyone in town who hadn't known him wished they had. I got calls from total strangers saying just that. And I bit my tongue to keep from replying, "Would you like to raise one of his children?"

Tom's whole life was theater, and he was the leading character—a little Falstaff, a dash of Don Quixote, a pinch of Don Juan, a little Huck Finn, and a lot of Tom Sawyer (always getting others to do his chores). His life had a changing cast. There were always several plots going on amid the ten children, the two ex-wives, and the innumerable friends and hangers-on.

Texas delights in characters like Tom, and they are getting scarcer each year, an endangered species that should be protected on some natural preserve, like the whooping crane or the golden-cheeked warbler. We mourn the loss of these legends and flavors.

So the morning after the funeral, people all over town picked up the paper to read Porterfield's account.

Tom Sutherland had the best funeral. It damned near matched his life. Where it came up short was that while it had its spontaneous moment of Sutherland poetry, profanity and humor, and even mystery, it was briefer and better organized than Tom, thanks to his older daughters.

Picture a big, full-bodied horseman of a craggy, noble bloodline reduced, after 79 years, to the confines of a pine coffin. A resplendent Mexican saddle and the worn cowboy hat and lariat that accompanied it at the foot of the coffin. Some in the audience, such as Lady Bird Johnson, were among the royalty of Texas. And then there were, thick in the middle of things, people still learning English from south of the border because Tom Sutherland gave them America. In return, a Nicaraguan couple helped Tom, who late in life found himself a bachelor with three kids still at home, keeping body and household together.

The spacious pews were filled with mourners who laughed as much as they wept as the eulogies were given.

The story went on to relate how Tom's college friend Bob Eckhardt, a former congressman, recalled surprising scenes that were the backdrop for their long conversations on virtually anything.

On one particularly memorable occasion, Bob told us, "I became aware, during an intense conversation, that several little girls, all naked out of the bathtub, had walked up his back and across mine as we hunkered there in talk." Tom was so absorbed in the subject that he never broke sentence as the little girls found the two men perfect substitutes for a jungle gym.

As one of many eulogists at Tom's funeral, I spoke about his total inability to fix anything, including a burned-out light bulb in a reading lamp. Once I dropped in on his disheveled home while he was reading by a flashlight fastened with black electrical tape to the lamp. I recalled how exasperated I had been, demanding, "What are you going to do when the flashlight burns out?"

He had answered with a grin, "I'm going to get a jar of lightning bugs and tape it on."

"My beloved brother," I said, "was the most inspiring, loving, and exasperating man I have ever known. Only Tom would have two ex-wives and ten children, ages fifty-five to eleven, in the same room and expect them to get along.

"But maybe we can. Maybe we can," I said, speaking not so much to the congregation as to myself, trying to find some measures of reassurance for what I was about to undertake.

The older daughters spoke with affectionate stories. Then strangers came forward. Wearing a worn and limp red dress, a woman known to no one turned out to be one of the street people who knew him. Once when he stopped to talk to her, he encouraged her to write poetry. She wanted to say that he got her started back to writing.

After nine eulogies, our cousin Sid Fly ended the service by playing his guitar and singing poems written by Tom.

It was just two months earlier that Tom, bloated and dying of heart disease, cancer of the lung, and a lifetime of misusing his body, summoned me home from my vacation in the Napa Valley of California because there was "a medical problem." I came and found that he wanted someone—namely, me—to take his two youngest—Mary, eleven, and Tommy, fourteen—

to live with me, at least until he got better. They
needed to enter school, so why not in my area of West
Lake Hills, Tom suggested, where there are some of
the best schools in the nation. Liz, who was to stay
with her mother, would continue at Austin High
School downtown. Unless someone took over, my
brother had warned, his kids were destined to be
unhappy dropouts, rootless and left to haphazard
living. Old and erratic as he was, Tom had been their
anchor and their bond.

"Someone has to care for these kids," he told me.
"You don't have any patience, Liz, but you *are* responsible."

I was chagrined at his arrogance once again. He
was willing to overlook my shortcoming—impa-
tience—if I took over this mammoth, who-knew-
how-long-it-could-go-on task.

I marshaled all the reasons against it—a busy
schedule, freedom to travel, and a rollicking circle of
partying friends. I had made my home a mecca for
writers and singers. I had my Bay at the Moon Society, a group of friends of "my age" (some in their late
fifties and sixties, more at seventy, and one pushing
eighty-five) who gather when the moon is full and we
are too. And I had pride in the fact that a few years
earlier I had gotten a marvelous contract for a book
on aging, and now I was still writing magazine arti-

cles, lecturing, and earning my own living despite a run-in with cancer. There were few gaps in my happiness.

I was also aware that my energy was declining. I was up early and eager to write or do the household errands, but by noon I needed a nap. I was now older and my body was ready for the "parts department"— down to one of everything. If he had asked me at fifty, it would have been bad enough. But I was seventy with one bosom gone, one deaf ear, a swollen arthritic ankle, and the weakest bladder in Travis County. I qualified for a handicapped parking sticker (not because of the bladder, though it relieved that humiliation more than once).

I valued being able to visit my own two children and grandson in Seattle and San Francisco, to rent a house in some cool summertime resort and share it with friends, to go anywhere I wanted, and better still to be able to accept speaking invitations all over the country that furnished me a comfortable living.

Even with my deep sorrow for my brother's plight, and my sympathy for the teenagers adrift in the family and the world, I had a sinking feeling inside that I was being overtaken. Money management in my brother's life was nonexistent. He could quote Polonius's famous advice at length: "Neither a borrower nor a lender be!" But he never took it to heart. Tommy's house must be sold.

The children's mother, Nancy, was facing an over-whelming situation. She needed time to try to work things out. School was in session, and the children needed a place to live and a school to attend.

As I lay awake worrying what was best and what was right, I kept remembering my own mother, whose house was never too crowded to share with needy kinfolks. I looked at those shy children who had grown up in loving chaos, tossed from school to school—it was a miracle they were making their grades. And so it came to pass as if it had been fore-ordained: Nancy would take care of the oldest, "little Liz." Tommy and Mary would stay with me.

Some of my own family tried to lobby me out of it, even urging my own faraway children to block the inevitable decision.

To the eternal credit of my son, Scott, and my daughter, Christy, they never joined in this counter-offensive.

We all pretended—Tom, the kids, and I—that the move was not necessarily permanent. Just until Tom got better. But of course we knew.

During the five weeks Tom lay dying and Tommy and Mary were with me, we were all overwhelmed by our emotions—getting used to the new school, the new house, and each other. Along with it all, I was trying daily to rally Tom's spirits, assuring him the kids were all right. We made short visits to see him.

It was apparent that he was rapidly declining. His legs were swollen. Thank God for Carlos and Anna, the Nicaraguan couple he had befriended. They were with him every day. As the time drew nearer, Hospice Austin arrived to help.

One day, I awoke with the strong feeling we had better get over to his house because it might be the last time we could see him alive. I called him, and his voice sounded so weak over the phone. I picked Tommy and Mary up at school and tried to control my voice as I told them it was time to go see their father. I think they sensed the finality of the day. Tommy told me many months later that he had an awful feeling in his stomach that this was the day he would lose his dad and he wasn't ready for it.

"Riding along," Tommy later recalled, "I glanced in the rearview mirror and I could see Mary's face. It was the face of a distressed child."

We were grief-stricken and tearful as we entered Tom's home this last day of his life and found Liz already there. I shudder as I remember that afternoon. Tom's clothes were being removed. Books were being taken off the shelves to store in another building to await distribution along with his large collection of guns and knives and saddles, which were in the living room. It was premature. Tom was conscious of what was happening. He could still see enough to be aware of the preparation for his exit from this world. Efficiency had taken priority over sympathy.

Tom knew we were coming, so Carlos and Anna had propped him up on the couch. The three children seemed so small and vulnerable, nestling against his massive swollen body, kissing him and saying good-bye. I hated having this important moment against a backdrop riddled with boxes being taken out of the house, clothes being draped over hangers, furniture being moved.

My brother hugged the children dearly, and Mary and Liz, tears streaming down their faces, hugged and kissed him over and over. Young Tommy turned away so his tears wouldn't show, then, shoulders straightened, turned toward his father, who put out his hand and said, "Good-bye, podner," and whispered into his ear, "You must always face up to what stands before you."

"His voice was so weary and weak," Tommy told me later, "that he barely got it out."

It was a strange feeling taking Tommy and Mary to my house that afternoon. There was a finality now that we all understood. What must they feel—looking at the aging aunt who would replace their aging father as their caretaker?

Sitting in the church at his funeral listening to the eulogies, I was overwhelmed by a sense of loss. We had lived across town from each other, but he was as close as the telephone and he could always come up with a perfect word change in my magazine stories or a line of poetry that fit. I delighted in his sense of humor, despaired in his total lack of organization and reality, and loved nothing better than a rainy evening when he escaped from his brood and cooked chili over my stove while we sipped margaritas with fresh lime.

He made margaritas and chili with ceremony, pulling out whatever knife he had—a red Swiss Army knife or just a rough-edged meat knife—for the lime and then the chili. He would rub a squeezed lime around the rim of the margarita glass and rub the rim in a saucer of heavy salt. His chili was perfect as he moved from cumin seed to garlic and onion to his taste. He had taught me a lot about cooking—always generous with lime juice, even in guacamole, for which he advised me to "always save the seed" to put in the middle of the bowl to keep the mashed avocado from turning dark. For pinto beans, you brought them to a quick boil, then set them aside for an hour before adding the salt pork and simmering slowly. You did that if you hadn't soaked them all night, which was better.

But I submerged my own grief and tried to comfort the bewildered trio of younger children as the service went on. Liz, oldest of the three, and Mary, the youngest, clung to each other and their mother. Tommy, the fourteen-year-old son, was by my side. He had been invited to be one of the pallbearers, but was too dazed to comprehend what it meant.

Then, at the cemetery, he asked, "What is it you want me to do?"

"I want you to go help bring your father's casket to the grave," I said. This was a whole new experience for him—death and the formalities of a funeral—but he headed down the hill where the casket was being unloaded from the hearse. There were plenty of pall-bearers, so the funeral director told him to just walk in front with the preacher. He did it with pride, tall and straight as a Scottish clan chief, leading the procession to the empty grave. That sight lives in my mind.

Because of Tom's lifelong fight for civil rights and his stint as the first executive director of the Good Neighbor Commission, he was eligible to be buried in the state cemetery, a rolling hillside of tombstones for Texas heroes and scoundrels. Tom would take his resting place near the grave of J. Frank Dobie and in sight of our great-great-grandfather, Sterling C. Robertson, who had helped General Sam Houston win the Battle of San Jacinto.

On this chilly September day a large assemblage of

friends and family stood there around the gravesite. Emmett Shelton, my eighty-seven-year-old neighbor and a seasoned storyteller, had kept his beloved bugle from Marine days next to his body to keep it warm (if it's warm, it is easier to play). After the final words, he put it to his lips and played "Taps" so clearly that even Tom's older daughters, who had objected to my insistence on it as "too militaristic," were pleased.

All ten children surrounded the grave. Tom had loved them all with the easy-come-and-easy-go nature that got him into the overpopulation business in the first place.

Porterfield's words summed him up: "Tom was an authentic lone ranger. Fame and wealth did not so much as wink at him. But what a picture he cut with horses, women, children, students, and compadres. All were drawn to him."

Later, we went home, my new family and I. We left behind us, on that Texas hillside, the lives we had known, and began to move together into an uncertain future. Liz looked back over her shoulder at her departing brother and sister. They returned her gaze. Surely it must have been hard on these youngsters to lose their father and see their family split up at the same time.

I missed the final touch that Porterfield used to end his story:

After all had left but the sextons who would cover the grave, a young blonde in fall slacks—about the age of a college student—got out of a red car and walked crisply to the maw that was about to swallow the remains of Tom Sutherland. The men stopped their work and discreetly stepped back. The young woman stepped to the lip of the grave and bent her head. She was still there as I turned my car into the drive and left.

There was certainly the implication that the young woman was a romantic friend. Ever the rogue, I thought. Tom's worn and dilapidated wallet was in my care, and a few days later, as I was paying the bills, I went through it for his identification cards and, lo and behold, there was an aged condom tucked away. He, having been an Eagle Scout, was always prepared.

3

Father of the Brood

A few days later, we had to go back to Tom's house one final time. A FOR SALE sign was already in front and it seemed to cast a pall on all of us, though we didn't speak of it. It was eerie and ghostlike to reenter this house, now emptied by death. I think we all felt as hollow as the house seemed, remembering how full of life and people it had been.

However disorderly and dysfunctional it had always appeared to my eyes, it was home to these children and the one they would remember most. Now, in disarray from the moving that had already taken place, it was only a skeleton of the Dr. Doolittle house it had been. The stacks of books leaning like the Tower of Pisa, because the bookshelves were filled, had all been packed in boxes and moved out to an empty rent-house on Tom's small ranch, where his nineteen Arabian horses were being sold off one by one. Remaining were two pianos in the rather small dining room. And the ever-present five saddles in the living room, poised on various pieces of furniture.

Mary and Tommy and I began to dig out their possessions to carry to my house, now that we knew it would no longer be just a temporary home: Tommy's voluminous collection of comic books, Mary's ice skates and other possessions. I noticed that Mary picked up the family picture albums with snapshots of her mother and father and other family members. There were family pictures framed and standing on her chest of drawers, and she gathered them up in her arms too. It became apparent to me that Mary was the most sentimental when it came to family. While she was not yet twelve, she had a family feeling that surprised me, considering the disjointed environment she had grown up in.

I was suddenly aware that I really didn't know my brother's children, except through the eyes of their proud father and our daily conversations and occasional visits.

Now, watching Mary purposefully dig in the clutter to find her things, I remembered that she had, at a younger age, been the one who got herself up early each morning and headed without breakfast for school to stand on a street corner in the safety patrol by seven-thirty. She had won the school spelling bee and gone to the city-wide competition, where she made it to the final ten before missing the word *terrain*.

As she visited her old house for the last time, she was silent and stoic, methodically going about her duties. I wondered what she was thinking, and my heart reached out to this youngest child, whose father had so often quoted her comments for to-the-point intelligence. I remembered the day she was born. Tom had called me excitedly from the hospital's birthing room, "Come on over and meet Mary Robertson Sutherland. She's a little beauty." (He had named her for our own mother, whom we adored.) I hurried to the hospital and held her when she was just two hours old, and stroked her soft baby-black hair and felt her cheeks. Now, almost a dozen years later, this child was growing into a beauty with blond hair, lovely features, brown eyes, and long legs. Already she was tall for her age, surprisingly graceful, and graced with wit. When she laughed, it was a spontaneous and contagious outburst.

I found that when we were discussing her father's irrational and hilarious habits, Mary's recollections were full of loving humor.

"Like the time Daddy arrived at the end of a garage sale and offered them thirty dollars for everything left, without even seeing it," Mary said with a laugh.

"He got it and it included some useless old scientific books predicting that one day man might get to the moon."

Tommy had finished gathering up stacks of comic books and wanted to leave and go buy the boxes that fit them. It was a good reason to exit, because remaining in this echoing house was making us all blue.

He put his hand lightly on Mary's shoulder. "Come on, Mary, let's go," he said. These two, just two years apart, were very close. When they were little and would go to the park to play, their father would always remind Tommy to "look after Mary." And he had.

Years before my brother passed away, I had gathered up a group of my nieces and nephews and my visiting grandson, Les, to spend the day at Sea World in San Antonio. Mary had wandered off. We searched for her for hours, it seemed, and no Mary. I was frantic because it was almost closing time. I called for help from the security guards throughout the park, but while they were looking, it was Tommy who guessed where she would be—sitting in the bleachers watching a water-ski show.

He hugged her protectively and softly lectured, "Don't wander away, Mary. We don't want to lose you."

She still sees him as a protector, her security blan-

ket, and when her brother happens to be absent, she
will invariably ask, "Where's Tommy?"

Some things we couldn't take at this time—
Tommy's well-used baby grand piano stood there
like a wooden island in the debris. We'd have to arrange to have it moved. The piano had been given to
the three youngest children by Carol Blodgett, one of
the many characters who dropped in at the house, a
songwriter with a big dog and a generous heart.

We left as soon as we got everything we could carry
into the car. When we reached my house, across the
city in West Lake Hills, we hauled things into the
guest house, which was across the yard from my
bedroom. This would be the center of their activities
for the future. For now both kids would sleep out
there. This allowed the least disruption to the main
house, where I lived, worked, and frequently enter-
tained. Besides, Mary wanted to be close to Tommy.
My house is spacious by most people's standards,
but there are really only two bedrooms, and I used
the smaller one as an office. In addition to the two
bedrooms there are a small enclosed sun porch, a
dining room, a den, and a living room. But none of
the rooms is overly large and the sixty-year-old
house sags a bit here and there (like its owner), and
most important it is one of those houses that "flows."
In Texas we call them shotgun houses—long and
narrow and not much more than only one room wide,

with each room opening onto the next. So there's not a lot of privacy.

The guest house allowed the children to have their own "space" (so important to kids today) and to be together. It's built of white limestone and sits on a terrace. It is mainly one big room, made cozy in winter by a rock fireplace. There is a shower bathroom, and glass sliding doors open the front of the bedroom/living room to a spectacular view of the city skyline and, on crisp winter mornings, a magnificent coral sunrise. Deer wander past, a sight that always surprises visitors, for from that window we can see the capitol dome and the University of Texas tower looming beyond the winding Colorado River. There are beds, a sleeper sofa, a chest of drawers, a large table used as a desk, and of course, a TV set, which already seems to get only one channel: MTV. This room adapts to many uses. I have rented it out in the past to scholars who came here to do research. I have used it as an extra guest room. Now it would be an all-purpose children's room. As Mary got a bit older I knew we'd have to have a different arrangement with more privacy for her. But for now this would do fine.

As a diversion that day from the upheaval, we set off to the mall to replenish a scanty wardrobe. In Tommy's case, he wanted jeans that were oversize and faded. I thought they looked like hand-me-downs from some giant, but he insisted they were his "style." Or no style, I thought, but kept my comment to myself. That much I remembered from being a parent the first time around. For Mary, jeans, T-shirts, and shoes as well as two kinds of shampoo and conditioner. We were hitting two hundred dollars and hadn't finished.

Next on the list was the grocery store, to let them pick their favorite foods. I had already filled the kitchen shelves, remembering how my brother had said, "Everything brought into this house is eaten." The first meal of our life together was fairly traditional—one meat, two vegetables, salad, and dessert—as it was supposed to be. But I felt their special selections would be solace, as food often is.

We have since looked back and talked about this "settling in" day.

"I was excited when we first came," Tommy recalled. "I was getting out of all the confusion at home. Your house seemed so light. There were three TV sets. Things were orderly and it was easier to get things done that I wanted to do. And the refrigerator was full.

"Sure, I miss my father," he added. And to my surprise, he began talking about grief. For a fourteen-year-old, Tommy dealt with his grief better than the rest of us.

"Our culture doesn't know how to handle death,"

he said to me. "We cry and feel sad but many cultures believe—and I believe—it means you are going into wider understanding—wonderful and limitless understanding. My father, a man of literature and a poet, would find that world all right."

I reflected to myself that my brother, the poet-professor, had passed from this world with some relief from his pain and, hopefully, a peace of mind because someone was shouldering his burdens. He would find his new home—his Place of Wider Understanding, as Tommy had called it—full of wonderment and free from the problems of everyday life. We, left on earth, had to carry on with the problems we inherited.

Tom left his children a memory of love and a colorful heritage and the useless but romantic paraphernalia of a time long vanished. And he left me with a new awakening of parenthood in the nineties.

A week after Tom's death, his ten children gathered together for what we called the Great Knife and Gun Show. The knives and an arsenal of guns he had collected were spread on benches around a tree. The game plan was to allow each of the ten children to walk around and see the various piles and speak up for a knife or two and a gun of their choice. If no one contested it, then it was theirs. It was a sunny day and the sister whose home and yard made up the distribution point had prepared a pot of coffee and some coffee cake. All was calm on the surface, but this was a tense first test of a division of property, however worthless to my eyes.

Tom left over a hundred knives, a couple dozen hunting knives and machetes, thirty illegal knives (the blade being longer than six inches), thirty unique and exotic or foreign knives collected from Africa, Spain, and Central and South America, and four or five swords: one from Spanish royalty, two from Japan, one from a French soldier, and one from a Filipino worker in a pineapple field.

And guns! My brother left at least thirteen rifles and seven handguns that he had kept in a red painted chest at the foot of his bed. Some were missing, it was quickly noted. The only guns left were rifles of lower quality. What had happened to the missing guns? We guessed that Tom gave the 12-gauge and AK-47 to Carlos to go fight in the war in Nicaragua. As far as I know Carlos is still somewhere down there fighting, hopefully for the people.

Nothing appealed to Tom more than imagining himself a cowboy, out on the frontier with his horse and knife for a companion, even though most of his life was spent in front of a blackboard as a teacher. Because he loved these implements of the Old West, he spent many hours introducing his son, Tommy, to the history of each knife. In an old hardwood box, he kept the knives in leather rolls, and he never tired of telling of their origins.

There was a knife from Spain, three from Mexico, and some that looked like they were Arabian, right out of "Ali Baba and the Forty Thieves." Often there were inscriptions. A favorite of my brother's was the knife whose handle was engraved in Spanish: "My love is in all the pretty horses."

I have never seen a nickel distributed between siblings without hard feelings. And so it was with these rusty guns and knives. It's surprising we didn't have a shoot-out as tension grew. All this was repellent to me, as someone who is more antigun than Jim Brady.

Tommy had just picked up the Bowie knife when one half sister walked over to him and started talking in a voice with which you would address a five-year-old, "Tommy, that knife really means a lot to me. I think you should let me have it."

Tommy, shy and even at fourteen a gentleman, yielded but mentally noted that no one had spoken up for the Bowie until he did.

Mopping up after death is always more extensive than one envisions. Three families were involved: Tom's first family, self-sufficient and withdrawing to their own worlds as rapidly as possible. Then there was his second family of three children, Tommy,

Mary, and Liz. And there was Nancy, his second wife, and her older children, by another marriage. Nancy frequently came back to visit his house and her children by both marriages who lived there.

Nancy's son, Steve, now twenty-one, seemed at a loss to know what to do next. Even after Nancy's divorce from Tom, Steve had kept in touch with his stepfather and in the final hours sat up for the all-night vigil. Steve was a good-looking Nordic type, a fair-haired young man. He could make something of himself if he had encouragement and a helping hand. I liked Steve, and we talked as often as I could reach him by phone. Finally it occurred to me that there was a Job Corps camp thirty miles away and maybe we could get him in and he would go.

Three phone calls later it was arranged and Steve began to show enthusiasm. This was to be one of the first small successes of this effort to move the lost family into productivity. Two years later, Tommy, Mary, and I went down to see Steve graduate and head to San Antonio to begin work at a printing company where his new skills as a binder and lithographer qualified him. He was a different Steve when he drove off for his first paying job, smiling and eager to begin a new life.

Again, I mentally thanked LBJ and the War on Poverty, which opened my mind to how it was possible to turn things around for people. The War on

Poverty had been one of the most exciting parts of my life. As press secretary to Lady Bird, I had often planned her visits to projects, especially Head Start programs and the Job Corps camps.

I remembered the story I had once told Steve about one experience I had when Lady Bird and I visited a camp in the mountains of Pennsylvania where troubled young men were being trained to operate heavy machinery needed in the construction trade. They had come from the environment of crowded tenements and shrieking sirens and the relentless noise of the city.

Conversing with one new seventeen-year-old corpsman, Lady Bird inquired, "What was the hardest thing about making your mind up to come here?"

"Getting on the bus and riding fifteen hundred miles in silence. The silence was scary. I almost turned back," he confessed.

"What made you stay?" I wondered aloud.

"I figure it's my last chance," he said.

How awful to be seventeen and having your last chance!

Encouraged by Steve's new lease on life at the Job Corps, the next effort was to get his mother, Nancy, back into college and into a job. I pored over the classified ads and set up appointments, but nothing moved. Weeks passed. Finally we heard about a major catering service that was hiring. Having been turned down before, Nancy wasn't eager to have that happen again, so I went with her to apply. But this time she was found qualified and given part-time work. When we walked out, her head was high and she was smiling.

I tell this only to emphasize the importance of taking steps, however small. I did little except push, phone, and shove. A death creates a lot of problems that must be solved by someone else, or they won't be solved at all. And my Methodism and Lyndon Johnson's training made me know that being your brother's keeper can bring results.

One thing about aging, you have flashbacks to another time, a moment when you learned a truth. I recall a vivid morning when the War on Poverty was shaping up. I was present at a meeting in the Red Room of the White House. Lady Bird Johnson and Sargent Shriver had put together some twenty experts from throughout the country to talk specifically about Head Start and the Job Corps, two key programs for youngsters and teenagers.

I don't remember who said it—but the words live. "The point here is to take human material that is potential waste and transform it into usefulness."

4

Back in
the Saddle Again

*M*eanwhile, getting the kids into school was a matter of tedious paperwork, collecting past grades at schools across town, finding inoculation records, and filling out form after form. It was worse than getting a passport. Already it was apparent that my personal office for writing and lecturing was becoming the Liz Carpenter Round-the-Clock Placement Service for Teens. I never knew kids today needed an appointments secretary, a medical consultant, and a full-time secretarial staff, but that's what it takes—for starters—to make things efficient for them. I figured that even at minimum wage, I was worth at least $16,426 a month. And that's a conservative estimate!

But the most important tasks were making them feel at home in the neighborhood and getting them into Hill Country Middle School (for Mary) and West-lake High (for Tommy). School today is a far cry from school yesterday and a very far cry from that of my own time—the day before yesterday. You don't have to worry about someone putting a girl's pigtail in the inkwell, but you do have to worry about every-thing else.

"Watch for lurking litigation!" Bill Bombeck, Erma's husband, told me when we talked about my situation. Bill used to be a school principal.

"Years ago if two kids got in a fight," he said, "I would yell 'Knock it off, fellas!' and they would. Today they would call a lawyer."

Another veteran of fifty years of teaching told me that in the old days a teacher worried and prayed that every child would show up because absenteeism affected your salary. "Nowadays it's different," she said. "It's gotten so rough that you worry that the kids will show up."

Before school opened, there were eyes, ears, and teeth to be checked. Supermom doesn't have a prayer compared to Super-Surrogate—Auntie Mame with a high-tech Rolodex. I had the handy tools at home and so I used them in rapid-fire order: two phone lines, two word processors, and even the fax machine were commandeered to make appoint-ments, store information, and send messages for the kids. My office at home had been turning out laugh-along speeches for such disparate groups as the National Mattress Association and the Geriatric Caretakers Association (which I contemplated asking for payment in services instead of money). Both kids were wide-eyed as they saw the details of their lives being put into the word processor with a Tommy file and a Mary file as we made notations of social security numbers, back-to-school records, and emergency phone numbers. There was also a manila envelope that kept the receipts for Doc Martens shoes (too high) and several purchases of ragged, "hip" jeans at local vintage shops with names like Flipnotics, Room Service, and Love Cat.

My command post for school entrance and check-in records would have done J. Edgar proud. But really, I should have stopped trying so hard and taken my calm and gentle mother's advice. "Just remember," she would tell us when we kids got demanding, "as Martha Washington always said, 'There is nothing in this world really worth worrying about.'"

I took her words at face value then, but years later when I got closer to national problems and now as I faced September, truly the cruelest month for mothers, I wondered where Martha said that. Valley Forge? Or when George stood up in the boat crossing the Delaware?

I also remembered that Martha's hair went completely white somewhere along the way. Luckily mine
already was.

I forgot it can be hard to go to a new school and find
new friends. My only experience was when I was in
the second grade and we moved to Austin, put our
letter in the church, and enrolled my oldest brother,
Tom, into the University of Texas. So many Texas
families did just this. When the oldest child was
ready for the university, your mother scooped the
family up and brought everyone to this education
oasis in Texas.

It was easier to make new friends then, too. Everyone was friendly, and so I grew up in the wholesome-
ness of neighborhoods, sidewalk games with the kids
next door, regular Sunday school, caring people, and
the intellectual excitement of a great university. We
could walk everywhere or take the streetcar for a
dime. There were no worries about gangs or dangerous companions, no drug dealers around the corner.
My younger brother, George, and I were trusted with
a strange hobby: collecting whiskey bottles near the
stadium after weekend football games. How my
teetotaling mother allowed it I don't know, but she
indulged us in bringing home scores of Four Roses,
Seagram V.O., and I. W. Harper's bottles because we
thought they were neat looking. Over four or five

years, we collected more than three thousand and stored them in an empty garage attic behind our home, each type lined up with its brothers. Kids all over town compared collections like baseball cards. It seems so harmless now, compared to Mortal Kombat, Street Fighter, and the other awful video games that occupy children's time after school these days.

At school, our teachers—all older than now—were easy and laughed a lot with us as they taught us our multiplication tables and helped us practice the Spencerian ovals and push-pulls that made for beautiful penmanship. My music teacher, Miss Pansy Luedecke, had a Victrola and many great operas on fourteen-inch disks that we would listen to. Two of our favorite compositions were *The New World Symphony* and "In the Hall of the Mountain King."

"Listen for the cymbals!" she would say as she put her hand to her ear and we did too.

While I was in high school, and editor of the school paper, there were speakers who came to the university forums, and for fifty cents I went to hear Will Rogers and watch him twirl his rope as he talked about New Deal politics in his gentle, chiding way. I also remember sitting spellbound to hear the most important newspaperwoman in the country, Dorothy Thompson, tell about interviewing Adolf Hitler and Benito Mussolini.

Much of that freedom of thought still lives in Austin. It remains a great town in which to live and raise kids, even though we now have crime in the streets and dope in the schools. I am horrified, but grateful too, that the police bring dogs to sniff the school lockers. (But how sad that it is necessary.)

The first day of school for Mary and Tommy came and we were ready for it. I was determined to get them there on time. I had pressed for dress-up clothes on the first day—something with a Peter Pan collar for Mary and a clean button-down shirt for Tommy, I thought, would be nice. I would even have settled for a polo shirt with a little alligator on it. Needless to say, I lost. So their clothes from the odd clothing stores were laid out, my car was gassed and oiled and the tires checked, and two alarm clocks had been set in case one didn't go off. I had also made a neighbor promise to call me at 6:30 A.M. as another backup.

It was a sleepy Tommy and Mary I hauled out of bed and pushed to dress, a procedure they followed like silent robots as I urged them to hurry. The breakfast table was set and ready for them. "I don't eat breakfast," Mary said as I shoved the orange juice and two kinds of cereal toward her.

I inspected them on the way out and handed over a brush and a comb for final touches. We were in the car before I had time to glance at the clock. It was seven-thirty A.M. We weren't due at school until eight-thirty and the schools were only ten minutes from my house. Today it took only five because there was no traffic yet.

Mary refused to get out of the car when we got to school because there was no one there. "It's still locked up," she said and she was right. So we sat . . . me trying to make cheery conversation while we waited five, ten, twenty minutes to see someone else appear. I walked her in and introduced her to the admissions people, spotted the principal and introduced her to him (which didn't particularly please her). I promised I would be back in front when school let out at three-thirty. Then back to the car and the same routine with Tommy, who hung back and refused to walk with me to the admissions office.

That afternoon, I was there by three P.M., the first car in front of the school, waiting for Mary. I had spent the day buying groceries, cooking a wholesome meal, and preparing snacks attractively arranged on a plate with a pitcher of lemonade.

Waiting in the car, I was exhausted, and when Mary finally got there, she had to wake me up at the wheel. In fact, she was giggling because it occurred to her, she said, that she had a CD called *Asleep at the Wheel.*

Mary had her books in hand, but she was also holding a large cello, taller than she was.

"I'm gonna take orchestra," she explained, "and the teacher told me to bring this home and practice." I couldn't wait. At least it was likely to be quieter than Soundgarden or Guns N' Roses.

We tried the trunk for the cello but it worked better in the backseat.

"Tell me all about school," I urged her as I drove toward Tommy's school.

No answer. Finally, "Well . . ."

"Was it fun meeting all the new kids?"

"Not really," she said.

"What was wrong with it?"

"Nothing really."

When we picked up Tommy and quizzed him, he was more forthcoming and enthusiastic about his new school.

"It was fat," he said.

"Who was? The teacher?"

"Nooooo," he said with forbearance. "The whole place. They have a theater, a football field, and I'm going to be on the soccer team."

So I learned that fat really was not something I had been fighting all my life.

We got home. Snacks were consumed. I urged them to go outside and get some exercise. Two seconds later they appeared back: Tommy with his skateboard and Mary holding up her bicycle.

"We need to go to the mall," Tommy said. "There aren't any sidewalks out here."

So we loaded the bicycle in the trunk and Tommy caressed his skateboard in the backseat, and we were back in the car in search of cement, a no-no in this hilly, environmentally fanatic part of town.

The next three weeks went along pretty much like this, and wherever I went around town I kept my eye out for nice big parking lots with acres of beautiful, flat asphalt and cement. I also learned to take along a book to read in the car and remembered that Jean Auel had said she wrote *Clan of the Cave Bear* and three other books about the Ice Age while waiting for her kids to come out of school in Portland.

As the days progressed, I let up on my penchant for being early to school. I guess it was a lifetime habit I had learned when I was a kid in Salado. In those days the Greyhound bus came through only twice a week, and if you weren't down at Norwood's store flagging it down as it sped between Austin and Dallas, you were stuck there for several more days. I saw many a disgusted traveler run with his suitcase down Main Street yelling at the driver to come back.

I was also beginning to eavesdrop on Tommy's and Mary's conversations, which provided an education all by themselves. One day they were sitting back near the stereo and I heard them talking about Led Zeppelin and Lemonheads and I thought it was some kind of teenage code.

"What is a lemonhead?" I wanted to know.

They looked disgusted.

"Lemonheads is a rock group," Mary said.

In an attempt to try to relate, I said lightly, "Are they the ones who sing 'Squeeze Me'?

"You're making that up!" Mary said.

I pressed them for more information on rock groups, and soon I was learning about Smashing Pumpkins and the Cranberries, which sounded like a Thanksgiving menu to me. And then there's White Zombie and Blind Melon and U2.

"By the way, Liz," Tommy said, "The tickets go on sale for U2 at the University Special Events Center Saturday, and some of my friends are going to take bedrolls and line up Friday night to be on time when the box office opens. It's gonna be a sellout. They want me to go with them. I have a bedroll. Can I?"

"Are you kidding?" I virtually shouted.

He looked disgusted.

"Look," I relented, "maybe I can arrange for tickets through the manager. He's a friend of mine."

"You can?"

It was established that we needed not just two tickets for Tommy and Mary, but two more for the friends. This was before word got out that "Aunt Liz can get tickets by making a phone call."

I called John Graham over at the Special Events Center and I tried the full ploy, "Look, John, I have this difficult situation. I am a seventy-year-old woman trying to get four tickets for the U2 performance. Not for me, mind you, for my nephew and niece, and I don't want them standing out all night to get them. Can you do anything for me?"

He sounded pleased and helpful. "Well, we do have some tickets reserved for special people, and since you're a distinguished alumna . . ."

I hardly let him finish before I sealed the deal and thanked him profusely. When I announced it to the kids they looked impressed with their old aunt for the first time. I hadn't figured that they would get on the phone and call every Tim, Dawn, and Hernando and brag, "We're going to the concert and are close enough to feel Bono's sweat."

After spending the evening on the phone, Mary came into my room and approached me with a plaintive look—warning bells sounded. "Liz," she started, "do you think you could get six more tickets for the concert?" It was the first time she really *asked* me for something.

I called John Graham back, more timidly this time. "Is it possible to get ten tickets?" I asked.

He sounded a little pained. "Look, Liz, you're not *that* distinguished." But he came through for me anyway.

From then on the kids read the coming attractions religiously. I pretended not to notice.

Here in my neighborhood of hills, I was happy that these kids were going to the best public schools in the state. I discovered a lot of changes, however. English has become language arts, home economics has become life management, and computer classes begin in grammar school. (I was sixty-five when I got my first computer.) All these expensive accessories, and yet it is a day of demons in and near schools—and I began to confront them through the horror stories of other parents. Yes, there are drugs in privileged neighborhoods, because that is where selling drugs is most profitable. Just as Willie Sutton robbed banks because, as he said, "That's where the money is," so the drug dealers hang out in affluent neighborhoods. Teachers today have to be vigilant about so much. Besides teaching, they have to cope with children who have warring parents or no parents, with children who get no discipline at home and children who get too much of the old kind of discipline, with a strap or a belt.

Thank goodness my only real demon was homework. The teachers here really pour it on because every teacher is competing for the Teacher of the Year award. Three or four hours a night over the books if you are zealous. It's not going to kill them but it may kill me. One night at nine-fifty Mary suddenly remembered she had a science project due the following morning. All she needed, she said, was a chunk of coal, a world globe, and a piece of wire. I had the wire and the whole world in my hand, but coal isn't exactly indigenous to this area, so we made a barbecue charcoal brick do. Mary got the wire and its charcoal satellite to school on time, but I was winded through the next day and strangely felt closer to NASA.

Another demon, as far as I was concerned, was detention hall as punishment for kids who walked into their classrooms barely a minute late. Once Mary and Tommy were late by two minutes because I had left the windows of the car open and it rained overnight. The seats were wet and had to be wiped up or we all would have shown up with wet bottoms. They got stuck with detention hall the following morning at seven forty-five, and that meant I had to get them there. Why can't they do detention on the honor system—let them get up early and sit in a corner at home? At least that way I could sleep in an extra half hour. Damn Texas's changeable weather! Damn principals who won't take wet car seats for an excuse! Damn my lousy memory!

Each day had a new challenge. I welcomed the Christmas break until I found that it may be godly for some but it is sheer hell for parents. Ten whole days when they slept until noon, watched TV all afternoon, and then wanted me to take them to wander the malls all evening so they could meet friends and play the game rooms. And I'll let you in on a secret, Nancy Reagan, you can't "Just Say No." Oh, I guess you could if you were the Marquis de Sade and wanted to be voted the Worst Surrogate of the Year, but I didn't. Malls for teenagers serve the purpose of the British pub or the village green. It's where you may meet anyone. The routine is simple: wander around with fast food in hand—corn dogs, nachos, Orange Julius, anything will do. So I deposited them in a mall with money for food and quarters to call home before eleven. This way I saw the late news, awaited the call, and then drove back to pick them up. When they didn't call, I was poised like Paul Revere ready to ride over "every Middlesex village and farm" to find them. Already, though, I was weary of this chauffeuring gig.

"Set out your expectations for them," I was advised by an expert parent. Thank God for computers and printers. I made a list and posted it on the family bulletin board and over every TV screen in the house to assure that it would be read.

TO: Whom It May Concern (This Means You!)
FROM: Liz (The Voice of Authority)
RE: The New Commandments

Like Moses, I feel compelled to deliver the rules for
the new millennium. If we're going to make it work,
here's what you need to do:

1. Answer the phone. Be polite and take a message.
    Ask for a phone number and assure them that I
    will return the call.
2. Show courtesy. When I'm not here you are the
    host for the house. Offer a chair or something
    cool to drink to friends who come by.
3. Stop sloppiness. Do not leave food, dishes, or
    glasses all over the house.
4. Keep the icebox tidy. Don't drink out of the new
    bottle if the old one isn't empty.
5. Spread up your bed each day. Even if it is lumpy
    it improves the looks of the bedroom.
6. Do not drop clothes on the floor. There are no
    hooks on the floor. Hang it up or put it in the
    laundry hamper.
7. Try volunteering. You could make a meal, offer to
    clean up after a meal, or sweep the kitchen floor.
8. Improve your manners at the table. Eat more
    slowly. Soup is to be seen and not heard. Watch
    the flying spaghetti. Don't pass a bowl in the

middle of taking a big bite. Make interesting conversation at the dinner table, but not with your mouth full.

9. Say please and thank you. Often.
10. And of course, grow in mind, heart, and spirit.

It was apparent from the moment I set foot at Mary's back-to-school night that I was the oldest member of the PTA—by years, decades maybe. Some people looked sympathetic, as they eyed my cane and assumed I was either a grandmother or maybe the speaker for the night. Everyone in the room was under fifty. All the parents were fashionably dressed and accessorized with their cellular phones. When I horned in on a group to eavesdrop on their conversation about discipline, I introduced myself by saying, "I have a child here."

They smiled politely but they seemed pretty suspicious. Maybe they thought I was there as a spy from the Gray Panthers to investigate tax dollars and the school budget. Or that I was angling to be Ripley's Believe It or Not's Oldest Living Mother of a Teenager. I don't think they ever bought my story. Afterward, when parents gathered in the lunchroom for refreshments and compared teenage problems, I continued to listen. Ye gods, two girls had been caught in the corridor looking suspicious, their purses searched (without a warrant, one parent noted), and found carrying a strange-looking group of pills. Speed-balls? The principal sent it for analysis at the Travis County Lab. How can this age group be filled with the perils of hazardous chemicals? But they are.

Another parent, anxious over the reports that her son kept his head on the desk in nearly every class-room, was worried.

"I don't think anyone can be that bored," she said. So she sent him off to a shrink "to talk about what bothered him."

The shrink called her back and told her that the kid never showed up but she owed him eighty dollars anyway. She made another appointment, and this time, she said, she became a stalker. "I'm not proud of it," she told us. "I waited at school at a safe dis-tance to follow him. He came out, got in the car, and headed for Thundercloud to get a roast beef sub, so I pulled up behind him and honked and waved. He pulled out in disgust but, no fool by now, I simply followed along until he reached the psychiatrist's of-fice, and there I sat, waiting for him and reading *Son of Sam*, which I recently checked out of the library to get tips on stalking. I'm an expert now and if any of you need advice, call me."

It was I-can-top-that night, and another mother excitedly jumped in to tell about having a group of twelve-year-olds over for a birthday party. After the dessert was served, the kids joined in a food fight, spooning ice cream across the room into a wall and throwing hunks of cake at each other.

Chalk that up to Hollywood again. These kids were mimicking John Belushi in *Animal House* by screaming "FOOD FIGHT!" Then the food flew across the room and against the wall.

"We sent everyone home! It was the worst experience of my motherhood," a still-sobbing mother said.

A couple took over, "Be glad it was only food! There was a teenagers' party in a very nice neighborhood near us. Unfortunately, the parents weren't there. When they got home at midnight, the wife's jewelry had been stolen. They sent out a letter to the parents of all the invitees, reporting the loss, and pointing out that it was sentimental jewelry, and if returned to the mailbox, no questions would be asked.

What happened? We all wanted to know.

"Nothing," the couple replied. "Not one acknowledgment from a parent, not even a sympathy note! Can you believe that in this neighborhood?"

I was getting more and more nervous about raising two teenagers.

I came home after the meeting, and before I got to the front door of the house I could hear laughter inside. What a nice sound to welcome me home. Mary was lying on her stomach with her legs in the air and holding a couch cushion between her feet while watching television. She was laughing at *The Simpsons.*

"Have you done your homework?" came out before I even had time to think about it. I guess my mothering instincts of thirty years before were coming back. She replied in the affirmative. When the show ended, she went to bed.

All was quiet in the house. Mary was asleep in the room next to mine and Tommy was out in his room.

In the middle of the night I woke suddenly out of a deep sleep. Beautiful music came from somewhere and it sounded like it was inside. I walked to the other end of the house and at the piano sat Tommy, head bent, fingers on the keyboard, playing with a quiet intensity. If I were a painter I would have called it *Musical Genius at Work.* I stopped for a moment and listened. He didn't realize I was in the room. The notes drifted comforting and soothing from the piano into the dark.

I turned from the room and went back to my bedroom, the soft notes following me into a dreamy sleep. Tomorrow morning the worries would start again, but for tonight my widow's house on the hill was alive with laughter and music.

5

《(∞)》

And Then
There Were Three

I spent a cold November afternoon looking
desperately for a couple of good Samaritans to pick
Tommy up from school and take Mary to a dental
appointment while I taped a television interview for
CNN and tried to make final arrangements for Erma
Bombeck's upcoming visit. A cowboy friend of mine,
H. C. Carter, dropped by with some firewood and saw
me in action. He drawled, "I don't think you should
have any more children, Liz."

But I did. Before long, we made room for my niece,
Liz, who was eager to come. The school nurse at Liz's
school called and reported that Liz, who was doing
badly at school, told her that she was depressed because she missed being with her brother and sister.
She felt that she had no real home. The nurse said
Liz was going to flunk her courses. I contacted Nancy

to find out if Liz could come over to stay for a while. They both seemed relieved. So here was Liz at my doorstep, head hanging down, and no smiles.

I remembered how tender she had been to her father during his last days when pain made him demanding and testy. She passed much of that time curled up in a chair reading, but when he bellowed for help she was the first to bring him water or go check on something. She did so without a complaint. If someone had carried his portable radio away, she would retrieve it so it would be there to soothe him. Or she would read aloud to him, which he loved and which would help him doze off. He had helped her rehearse for her role in *King Lear* at school, and he liked nothing better than for her to practice the lines for him.

I knew Liz was probably here for the duration, and it was important to keep her last two years of high school from being a disaster. She couldn't go back to Austin High—the classes were just too big and she felt overwhelmed with all the other changes going on in her life. Westlake High, where Tommy went, wouldn't have been any different.

When I broached the idea of her going to a smaller private school, she jumped at the chance. It was going to cost me plenty—at least two speeches' worth (two top-dollar speeches)—and it meant more driving, since Kirby Hall, the school in question, was ten miles away, in the opposite direction from Mary and Tommy's schools. But the classes had only ten or twelve students in each and the teachers had time to give each student personal attention. It would solve her education crisis.

My housing crisis, however, only got worse. For a while Liz slept on the couch in my dining room and we rolled up the sheet and covers when anybody came to dinner. Some of my primmer friends raised their eyebrows at the thought of all three kids sleeping in the guest house, which is what they preferred. One wanted me to put up a screen to separate the girls and the boy, like the blanket between Claudette Colbert and Clark Gable in *It Happened One Night.* I listened but only for a while. And remembering that I'd grown up on a sleeping porch shared by a variety of cousins of both sexes well into my teens, I simply said, "To hell with it," and let them all move in to the guest house. I never thought seriously about the screen, but I didn't exactly broadcast the new arrangement to my friends either.

I wish I could say the kids all lived together happily forever out there, but like all teenagers they squabbled and bickered over T-shirts and swiped each other's socks. The first one up was the best one dressed. And that's not saying much. As time went on, the beds in my house became fruit basket turnover and everyone slept where it was most convenient. And on weekends when their friends were here there was no room at the inn.

My house was strained to the limits. I'd bought it for myself and a guest or two. Now it had to stretch to four—or more. It was a house set up and decorated with bright, flowery chintz patterns and light fabrics. But now, with three teenagers, dining-room chairs that were supposed to last for the ages began breaking. Someone had tilted in them. The kids had been used to eating in armchairs rather than at a dining-room table. Footprints and smudges were everywhere. My home—my castle—was being dripped on, spilled on, and broken here and there. I estimated about three thousand dollars' worth of breakage in the first few weeks after their arrival. But I figured the careless flying arms and legs of growing kids went with the package. How right, I thought, was the grandmother who said everything should be painted black until the children have left home.

I became a slave to a schedule and enforcing it for three children, perhaps too harshly, but as my brother had pointed out, patience is not my forte.

Liz recalls how shocked she was that meals were served at the same time each night and all had to wait until I said the blessing. Homework had to be done and bedtime wasn't fiction.

I stayed up all night planning and reading *TEEN Is*

a Four-Letter Word and *When Helping Them Is Hurting You.* I knew they needed discipline, but discipline was wearing me out.

I must have looked battered and haggard because my friends began offering more advice than casseroles. I could have gone to the penitentiary if I'd followed all the suggestions about how I should cope:

"Beat them with your cane."

"Shortsheet their beds."

"Teenagers are like wild animals, wandering around all night, peering at you from behind their doors. Put them in a cage."

"Withhold their allowances. Withhold food."

Most of this came from childless friends. Or friends who only had undisciplined dogs.

I shot back defensively, "Does anyone realize how much energy it takes to administer justice? No wonder the United States Supreme Court takes off from May to October. They must be exhausted after seven months of deciding what is fair. Justice is fine if you are a statue and blindfolded and all you have to do is hold up a scale."

Ironically, these drastic suggestions made me more sympathetic with the kids. The whole world was against them, and so I just couldn't be. I sought professional advice. We set up a family conference with a psychologist who was suppose to be good with teenagers. One glance and I knew why. He looked like a teenager. He had a ponytail and wore Reebok shoes. I remembered seeing him at the Whole Foods Store. But he did give us a chance to air our feelings and we all felt better afterward. I decided that instead of sending the kids to a psychologist I needed help more than they did.

I had never been to a shrink, so a psychotic friend made the appointment with her lady psychiatrist, who would see me at the end of each day, the only time she had an opening. And for six sessions I talked through my feelings. It was pretty dramatic stuff, spellbinding drama I thought. It was really insulting, then, that the psychiatrist kept dozing off as I talked. I can't stand audiences like that. At the end of each session, she would give me a line, a thought . . . "something to hang on to," as she put it. Maybe she had been praying for me. Anyway on the sixth session, I ran out of things to say and told her that. Besides, her maxims were somewhere between bumper stickers and fortune cookies.

"Fine," she said, "I think you are going to feel better. Here is my home number in case you need me." I never did. Her wisdom was to lead me, without my knowing it, to think and talk about my problems and see the answers more rationally.

But in the months ahead, despite the fact that she had done the unforgivable and slept through my tales of woe, I had to admit her daily parting words were helpful in adapting to my "new situation," as she had called it. I promised to try to be more patient about the noise and the looks of teenagers, specifically their music and their dress code (or lack of it). Their music, if you can call it that, was getting louder and louder. I tried to be tolerant. These kids couldn't spend ten seconds in the house or even in the car without slipping in a noisy hard-rock cassette. Thank God for a hearing impediment. But even with my bad left ear, the music was too loud.

"Down, Tommy, turn it down," I said in what I hoped was a mild-mannered voice.

I argued for something more lyrical.

"When I was a teenager, songs had tunes and words. My generation depended on the weekly Hit Parade to hear what was hot. Frankly," I explained, "I have a hard time understanding the appeal of some group called Jane's Addiction or Alice in Chains. Really, Tommy, any song that says, 'Do it, do it, do it,' is lousy advice if I ever heard it."

But Tommy has learned how to get to someone who cut her political teeth on the Great Society, who sang with Fanny Lou Hamer as we campaigned in Mississippi, and who personally knew two out of three of the namesakes in the folk song "Abraham, Martin, and John." (At least, I don't think Lincoln and I ever crossed paths. The kids would probably swear we were the same age, though.)

"Listen to this one. It has a message for freedom and justice," Tommy would argue. Or, "But that's a song of a woman seeking an equal place in this world."

So we compromised. I listened to their music on the way to school, and Tommy would accommodatingly switch to my romantic stuff for the drive home. "Have some consideration," he would admonish Mary when she tried to switch the music to the noisy Nirvana.

I found myself showing off my contemporary new knowledge to my friends and repeating Tommy's words: "Listen to the plea for freedom and justice."

The more I listen and the more I watch kids gravitate automatically to the stereo, the more I realize that music is an escape for them. Music can shut out a dysfunctional world. It's their pressure valve for anger.

"But why do they play it so loud?" I said in a long phone conversation with my son, Scott, who has, at forty, gone back to guitar playing. I find myself seeking Scott's advice more and more. After all, he has a teenager, my grandson, Les. And he was a teenager a lot more recently than I.

"You gotta understand this, Mom," Scott said, "if you want to find the difference between their music and yours. Yours in the thirties and forties was romantic. Music today is visual and physical. The kids turn the music up so they can actually feel it. It is sensory . . . well, yes, sexual."

I didn't think I could ever get used to their music, so we moved the family stereo to the Children's House (once the guest house). This giant room took the speakers, and I didn't have to listen to the sound. I got Mary earphones for her CD player so she could make her own choices wherever she was in the main house with me and to avoid the bedlam when three teenagers each wanted their own favorite record going.

Along with the stereos, we moved my small piano and Tommy's guitar and speakers to the guest house. Tommy managed to play them all at the same time. So it became a music room in addition to a bedroom and a gathering place for everyone in Texas under eighteen.

There were other changes. I was back into cooking as I had not been for thirty years and had to relearn the demands of the bottomless pit teenagers seem to own. I am a good cook and I enjoyed seeing them relish a good meal on the table, where I also tried to extract conversation and teach table manners. They ate. My kingdom, how they ate, and alas, so did I, as I kept the icebox filled and the meals tasty.

More relaxed, I even began to understand what fashion meant to them and accepted their opinion that the best jeans are the scruffiest jeans. Most hoboes wouldn't have worn what Tommy and his friends wore. I called them "porno" jeans. They were fraying at the knees and even more vital parts. It was high fashion to have them patched with bandana fabric. Tommy, who liked to be original in the couture world of patched pants, wanted his patches in the family plaid. Luckily we found a swatch of the Sutherland plaid and then I discovered why he had wanted the family fabric. Tommy had remembered that our clan motto is *"Sans Peur"* ("Without Fear"). He got a kick out of making this fashion statement from a patch in the crotch.

The girls, Liz and Mary, wore shorts, and the more frays of string, the better. At first I was appalled. But I vaguely remembered that back when saddle oxfords were popular, we would age them before wearing by smearing them with mud stains so they wouldn't look new. So maybe a few intentional tears in their jeans weren't so awful after all. Their T-shirts were plentiful, but they stuck to two or three all year long—washing them out for the next day. Mary liked an arty T-shirt—a Monet from the garden at Giverny. Two other favorites promoted popular rock bands, Nirvana, naturally, and the Unconscious. Liz wore one that said SIN-É, which means "that's it" in Gaelic. It is sold by an Irish café of that name in New York. For dress, she would switch to flowers with a rose on the collar.

When we went shopping, they let me know emphatically that no one wears short sets and matching socks. "That was the early eighties!"

Tommy was more patient with me. "Every teenager has to express his individuality," he explains.

I was learning to be amused by these habits and to be more relaxed about everything. I began to understand that furniture can be cleaned, broken chairs can be fixed, and loving words do help. My home became our home. It really pleased me to come home one day and find them stretched out on my bed watching television. I told myself it was because they felt closer to me, but in the back of my mind I was slightly suspicious that they were there because my TV set was the largest one in the house.

Meanwhile, I am conscious of the tug of war between age and youth. I take some perverse solace in the fact they will get older—a lot older. Alas, I won't get any younger.

Some days I feel that aging is overtaking me. While I share my home with three teenagers, I share my body with a multitude of doctors. They have divided me up into more parts than the former Soviet Union, and I have a busy schedule keeping up with the appointments to keep in reasonable shape.

It was my local ankle doctor who made me realize just how specialized and impersonal medicine has become. He was young enough to be my grandson. I know this because I knew his grandfather and his father. Picture this: My grandson-doctor gets on this tape recorder like he is talking to all three networks and CNN and gives the most boring and insulting description of my condition right there to my face.

"Mrs. Carpenter is obese with boggy synovium in the left ankle. Films show degenerative changes involving the left ankle with joint space narrowing and hypertrophic changes particularly along the tibiotalar and fibulotalar joints on the left."

"For God's sake," I told him, "is that all? Can't you say something flattering . . . like a dynamic, sexy woman who knows life at its fullest?"

He was back on the machine in a minute. "Mrs. Carpenter *says* she is a dynamic, sexy woman."

Talk about not sticking your neck out!

I, on the other hand, think that in order to protect your interest, you have to give generously to medical research. So, for several years now, I have been practicing the give-for-good-luck policy. Every time I get one of those envelopes soliciting money to prevent some awful disease, I pick out the ones that I am most likely to get—cancer, heart, kidneys, stomach worms—and send them a small check. I figure if I give, God will protect me from that particular ailment.

The other day there arrived in the mail a letter from

the Alzheimer's Foundation. Yes, I thought, I am now in that "Big A" age bracket. So I got my checkbook, sat down, and opened the envelope to write a check. Behold, it was a receipt and a letter thanking me for the fifteen dollars I had sent two weeks before.

6

Husband Wanted

*H*eeeelllp! What I need is a husband. Anyone's husband. Well, maybe not a husband so much as a male partner who would take on half of the tasks of shopping and driving kids to and from school, watching soccer games, delivering Mary and her friends to a school dance, and making these teenagers more responsible. Isn't that the inevitable mother's prayer?

I haven't done this kind of stuff in years, and it nearly wore me out the first time around.

Maybe a classified ad would find someone. My sleepless hours in the middle of the night were spent composing such an ad.

Wanted: Experienced widower who has raised one family and is ready for another. Must be

strong in mind, body, and calculus. Able to tolerate loud music. Severe hearing loss acceptable instead. Must like to shop for groceries and blue jeans. Own toolbox for repairing broken chairs, lamps, and screen doors helpful. Know how to extract daily chores from teenagers. Even-tempered, good-humored, and healthy. Willing to share home with a woman of sound mind and unsound body. Only licensed drivers need apply. Marine Corps training a plus.

In the absence of a husband, I found myself summoning help from anywhere I might get it: God, Allah, Buddha, Mohammed, Moses, Shirley Mac-Laine, Jimmy Swaggart, Ann Landers, Oprah. Is anyone out there?

Friends called to inquire, "How are you doing?" and came by to drop off cookies or casseroles. But the problem was that everybody left after fifteen minutes and here I was back on my own—me and three teenagers, and a lot of things that needed to be done. I was still the only driver (Liz had never learned and Tommy was too young) and the only person who did chores. I couldn't believe how many things would occur to me to do and how nothing would occur to them to do. But then I had to remember that no one had ever asked them to help before. Discipline was not their father's forte.

It is hard now to remember how tough those first few months were. We were virtually strangers to each other. I was trying to make it work, they seemed to be just waiting for what might happen. And I still had to keep working to earn a living—writing magazine articles, making speeches, answering the incessant phone. Once again I was thankful my office is in my home. It meant I could do the morning chores and go to work immediately—most days in an old blue bathrobe.

Typically, I approached my parental role with grim determination, as I tried to get a routine going: wake the kids up; get dressed; drive them to school; hit the grocery store; buy supplies; prepare snacks and supper; drive back to school to pick them up; prepare more food; crack the homework whip; more food; collapse (often before them). What is it Roseanne Arnold once said? If the kids are alive at the end of the day I figure I've done my job. I'd make it "If they're alive and have had five full meals and seventeen or eighteen snacks." I was busier than a long-tailed cat in a roomful of rocking chairs. Hopefully I would find four hours during the day to keep up with my professional workload.

Each morning was the same. My ringing alarm clock and firm voice (my own children had claimed that I woke them up like Captain Bligh in *Mutiny on the Bounty* shouting orders, "Off with the pajamas!

On with the shoes! Find your *clean* jeans!") would wake the dead, which on some days seemed like a preferable alternative. My first alert was a seven A.M. call: "Start moving. Put on your clothes." Three sleepy groans.

I waited ten minutes. Second call. "This is your friendly weather station. Temperature is eighty-three degrees. Sunny skies. I want to hear you moving."

And in ten more minutes, "If you aren't in here in five minutes, you're going to walk to school without breakfast!"

I was rapidly discovering that there was no time for me and very little freedom for fun. I became more isolated from friends my own age, who thought they shouldn't interrupt me from my busy task of keeping the kids on schedule. This was the Structure Period that the books talked about, but I was getting more structure than they were. I felt hemmed in, and in turn the kids couldn't believe what was happening to them. The friends who sympathized were confident that I would succeed. One even said, "At sixty-five, you lived through a mastectomy, a three-month book-selling tour, and judging the Ugliest Pickup Truck in Texas Contest in one-hundred-degree heat. You ought to be able to handle these kids. Hang in there."

It was Emmett Shelton, my wise and aged neighbor, who gave me the best advice. "You've got to think of it this way, Liz. There is a river of shit out there that you've got to swim through, and after you do it, you'll be okay." I'm still swimming, but I am hopeful.

The kids were beginning to get the picture. Instead of midnight they had to be in bed by ten-thirty P.M. . . . and they were. I first noticed it when little Liz came in one night and politely asked if she could stay up late to watch David Letterman because she wanted to see "Stupid Human Tricks." I was so overwhelmed by the request I immediately said yes, without thought of the possible side effects of seeing a full-grown man stuff himself in a dryer.

So dedicated was I to the bugaboo of homework that mostly I was coming through more like Aunt Polly than Auntie Mame, and I didn't like the image. But I was determined not to fail.

And I was adjusting to the balancing act and rhythm of life as I had known it with my own children when I had husband, job, two kids, LBJ, and the White House to juggle.

I called them up, Christy in San Francisco, Scott in Seattle. "How did I do it?" I asked. "Was my career traumatic on you? Do you have any hidden psychological problems?" I wondered if they were still sucking their thumbs or wetting their beds.

No, they'd had a great old time growing up, but it had affected me—in the head for the most part.

"You forgot things, Mom. You were spaced out," Scott said. "Remember the time you brought the wrong dog home from the vet?"

In my opinion this could have happened to anyone. But I remembered what has become a family legend. We had this fat dachshund named Mitzi. And she'd been at the vet for two weeks because there wasn't time for me to pick her up. When I did, I was handed this small, skinny dachshund, and I was horrified. All the way home, I kept saying, "Mitzi, Mitzi, I am soooo sorry. I feel terrible. It's all my fault."

She wouldn't even look at me. When we arrived home, the kids came tumbling out of the house and I lifted the skinny dachshund down out of the car. Both of them shrieked at the same time, "Mommy, that's *not* Mitzi!"

I ran into the house and called the vet. "Do you have a very fat dachshund there?"

He went to look, and then came back to say, "Yes we do."

"Well that's *my* dog, Mitzi. I'll bring you back the one you gave me."

He never did seem remorseful. I certainly was, but I'm not sure the kids ever forgave me. Clearly they never forgot the incident.

My daughter, Christy, brought up another exam-

ple of my zany lapses during motherhood in the Dark
Ages—the forties and fifties.

"Remember the night before Easter when you went
by a landscape place to get Daddy a present for the
garden, the statue of Saint Francis of Assisi? Well,
you were running on eight cylinders as usual . . ."

It began coming back. I remembered hurrying into
the shop and seeing all these small statues of a man
with long hair and sandals. I grabbed one up (I'm
afraid by the neck), paid for it, and was out in the car
and headed home. When I got home, again the kids
came running out and I showed them what we were
going to give Daddy.

"That's not Saint Francis," Christy said. "That's
Jesus!"

I was really chagrined and considered turning
around and exchanging him, but we had to keep him
of course. You just can't take Jesus back.

And the little statue is still with me. Never have I
needed him more.

7

A Grand Canyon Generation Gap

*I*f having children in the fifties was the Dark Ages of Motherhood, I had regressed to the Ice Age. I was too demanding, it seemed, and the three kids remained shy and distant. We didn't talk enough or understand each other.

I simply had not anticipated that meshing two worlds together would be so hard. Our generation gap was more than a gap. It was the Grand Canyon with more than half a century's difference in discipline, in morals, in music, and in a sense of history. Ye gods! It dawned on me that I was born not just before the space age, but before airplanes. I could remember when radio came to our little town of Salado, and my grandmother did not believe that we could turn on the black box and hear someone speaking sixty miles down the road at the state capitol.

Just how far apart our ages were was brought home to me when Mary kept complaining about being bored. "I haven't done anything for two days," she said.

"When I was your age," I suggested, "I read Nancy Drew, or played Michigan, or made fudge."

"But, Liz, when you were my age was sixty years ago!" she shot back.

I did the necessary mathematics and she was right. But no adult has ever been able to convince a teenager that he or she was once a teen. It would be much easier to describe figure skating to the nomads of the Sahara.

My world at seventy was most comfortable around people whose memory went back to Roosevelt— Franklin, not Theodore—or at least to JFK. My generation was shaped by the Depression, which makes us cut the lights out as we leave each room, eat every bite on the plate, and save string. A lot of my friends can't bear to throw a magazine away, not just their 1930 issues of *National Geographic,* either, but back issues of *Collier's* and *Boy's Life,* and the *Pathfinder,* which by now are so old they have almost become valuable collectors' items. Their garages, attics, and basements have become fire hazards. We still can't throw anything away, so we shuffle it around or frame the most sentimental trash and hang it on the walls.

Those of us born before the sixties were also shaped by Sunday school and two-parent homes where Mama stayed home and cooked and sewed while Daddy went to work. Madonna was a term reserved for the most chaste of women. I was in for a big awakening as I met teachers and parents at the PTA. I also met lots of single parents, men as well as women, and other kinfolks like me, drafted to raise children.

For Mary's twelfth birthday, she wanted a party. She knew eight girls—at least she knew their first names. These kids live in a one-name world. So we had to research the rest of it. This was an eye-opener for me. Out of the eight girls, only one came from a traditional home. Fathers were raising them. Grandmothers or aunts also got the call. Or they had to be juggled between divorced parents on schooldays and weekends. It took fifteen phone calls to clear everyone for a birthday party of eight.

Every day I woke up to stare across the generation gap. This generation—these teenage kids, mostly children of hippies, yuppies, boomers—is shaped by television, CDs, VCRs, and MTV. I call them the Remote Generation, since they always seem to have some remote control in hand. In some cases, their parents are still into pot or suffering guilt because they once had been. I watched some indulgent parents who wanted to be "pals" with their children and wouldn't take a firm stand on anything. If they became authority figures, they feared their children wouldn't like them.

In other cases, the child-parent relationship is about as tranquil as a combat zone. Many of the friends of Mary and Tommy, for instance, are living with the tension of divided affections between divorced parents.

As I watched this and overheard some of the phone conversations, it was not difficult to see that the country may be getting a new supply of skilled diplomats, practicing their peacekeeping missions at home. As divorce rates rise, these kids grow up yearning for peace in their own homes, cringing from fighting between parents or trying to escape from it with loud music or even meditation. Am I being too optimistic to think that today's turbulent homes may ultimately rally us into a greater effort for peace in general? Already, we see leaders emerging who try harder than past generations to prevent war. In another decade or two, is it too much to hope that one "plus" of the single-parent homes will at least pay off in a greater effort toward reconciliation? Some schools are foresighted enough to teach conflict resolution, and the kids respond, teachers tell me. During my brother's divorce from Nancy, young Tommy, only six then, would say, "I just want everyone to be happy." Such a plaintive plea!

I am learning many other heartening things from today's teenagers. I mustn't be surprised when they bring home a best friend who turns out to be of a different color. Most kids are color blind unless they have been carefully taught to hate. Parents must be color blind, too, in fact and not just theory. This generation may lead us away from the racism of past generations, and that is a journey we all need to take.

To an aging feminist, kids today are also gender blind in a most rewarding way. I notice that male and female friendships can develop without sexual overtones. And, males—Tommy and his crowd, at least—don't hesitate to enjoy poetry, art, museums, music, theater, and ballet in a way that would have been considered slightly "sissy" in my teenage times. Today, grown men don't only eat quiche, they make it! They also can cry openly. Even President Bill Clinton can be seen shedding tears and the world doesn't crumble.

And it's a whole new scene in sports. Our female governor leads the pack in attending sports events, especially women's sports events. A few years ago the University of Texas men's sports program had a lean year on wins: none. It was the Lady Longhorn basketball team that saved the day by winning all of its games. Texas fans like to win, so on any given night an arena full of "bubbas" buy the hottest tickets in town and cheer the national champions on to victory. The female players are given the same kind of hero status as some of the great football players.

I became more aware of things going on around me. The kids were learning too. But apart from the positives—and I have a habit of seeing them and brushing over the negatives—I slowly began to realize that drugs were not just a headline and statistic from across town but were right here in my neighborhood and in every school in town. I tried talking about the situation in the schools Tommy and Mary were attending, but there was not much feedback.

Dinner conversations were picking up, however, and it wasn't only my initiative. Thanks in great part to Liz's arrival at this house, there was a variety of conversation because she was older, less shy, and an avid reader. She grabbed anything in sight that was printed. She devoured the underground newspaper called *The Austin Chronicle* and would talk about current issues or movies at the dinner table. Mary began discovering there is life away from the TV set. Not much, but some.

Tommy developed a new interest in homework, and I spent a lot of time at the computer with him dictating to me. Slowly we began to get to know each other and adjust.

There remained difficult days when I knew why boarding schools had been invented, but more and more I began to realize I wasn't Supermom and I couldn't be Super Surrogate. The word *surrogate* is such a painfully inadequate and scientific word. It sounds like you are just below warden. What would the right term be? Guardian, Custodian, Keeper of the Kids, Tyrant of Teenagers?

"Look, Liz," my brother George, always a level adviser, said, "quit punishing yourself. You are doing the best you can and, after all, you didn't have them as they were growing up."

So I quit trying for perfection (a bad habit of Virgos) and became more philosophical. I was increasingly interested in them and the whole teenage scene, however trying it could be, and I began treating this experience as I would have back in my news-gathering days. What makes teenagers click? The story opened up for me as I applied my reportorial skills, analyzing the five *w*'s and the *h* of journalism days, the what, who, where, when, why, and how. The process was not only intriguing but enlightening.

I began to see the teenage years in the whole, and then apply it to my charges. I decided the teens are a time of stops and starts—physically and emotionally. It may be the most volcanic time of life. Take Tommy, whose rapidly growing muscles are the reason he knocks over chairs and has to kick a soccer ball around, even if he's indoors. One day he decided to chase a herd of deer that were grazing happily on what's left of my grass. They ran, and one of them panicked as they passed the living room and leapt against the plate-glass window, sending shattered glass all over the floor.

I got home about three minutes after the last deer had disappeared down the hill. Glass was all over Tommy's inherited piano. We found a piece of plywood and Tommy propped it up against the hole.

"How did you decide to chase deer?" I asked.

"I just felt rambunctious," he replied. "It didn't hurt the piano."

"No, though it would have if you'd been playing 'Afternoon of a Fawn.' "

Tommy thought that was pretty funny. I continued to press for more facts.

"How big was the deer? Was it a baby?"

"No, it was a teenager." He smiled slyly.

"Well, that figures," I said, and we both laughed, glad that the deer escaped even though bleeding.

What bothered me was that Tommy still hadn't said he was sorry, and I told him so.

"Who do I say it to—the deer?" he asked.

"How about *me*," I replied, "I'm the one who has to pay for fixing it."

"Well, I didn't do it on purpose," he replied.

On days like this one, he really reminds me of his father—maddening, but lovable.

In fact these three kids have surely inherited their father's sense of justice. Tom worked his whole life on improving our country's relationship with Mexico. He was NAFTA before NAFTA was cool.

One Monday night—the night nothing comes between me and my TV—Liz, Mary, and I were flat across my bed watching *Murphy Brown*. Tommy came home from soccer just ravenous and joined us in front of the television. Slushing down a big bowl of shrimp creole and rice, he began, "Something happened at school today." He doesn't usually start a conversation about school, I have to drag any bits of news from him. But he said, "The teacher [Miss Hutchinson] got mad at me because we were talking about Columbus and I said Columbus is a bastard."

"He is!" Liz interjected. "I can't believe how egocentric the Europeans were coming here thinking they owned this land. What right did they have?"

"They wanted land and gold," Mary joined in. "Why do we have to celebrate him anyway? He really didn't discover America. Just figured out how to get here from Spain."

"That's what I mean," Tommy said. His anger was rising over this injustice and apparently it had in class, too, because, he reported, "Miss Hutchinson got mad when I said 'God damn it.' She is very religious and Republican and she is always making these cracks about Clinton."

All three of the kids were more agitated than I had ever seen them. They felt angry on behalf of the lost Mayan civilization centuries ago and the Native Americans of our own land. I wasn't sure what to say to these teenage revisionist historians.

I began by saying, "You know, your father really knew a lot about explorers and admired many of them, particularly Cabeza de Vaca, who got shipwrecked off the Texas coast. When his party was washed ashore, they were met by Indians. Cabeza de Vaca was really tall compared to the Indians—six feet and more. He was brought before the chief and somehow the chief communicated to him that his life would be spared if he saved the chief's son, lying ill with fever.

"Your father told me himself how Cabeza de Vaca wrote in his journals to the king, 'Not knowing what to do, I made the sign of the cross.' Fortunately the boy lived and Cabeza de Vaca made his way across Texas guided by an Indian woman."

About this time, the theme for *Northern Exposure* started and we all turned our attention back to the television. Tommy was calmed down from his anger about Columbus and picked up his big soccer bag and headed for his room.

The next morning, I put a magazine article about the Maya on the breakfast table, along with my meditation book opened to a good passage on peace and harmony and using the Isaiah quote, "Come let us reason together."

I don't know whether any of them read it.

"You might think about apologizing to Miss Hutchinson for your outburst," I offered as we drove to school.

He opened the door to get out and stopped for a moment, "Well, I guess it *is* her classroom, but what about my right of free speech?"

I don't know if he saw my point, or was just buttering me up so he could lobby hard for a car, even though he was still more than a year away from the legal driving age. He reaches for freedom the way developing countries do. (This may be farfetched but I began to feel closer to Aristotle. Maybe I don't need a husband. Just a little more Aristotle.)

8

Ed McMahon, Where Are You?

*E*ven Aristotle worried about happiness and how to have the good life. My happiness is interrupted by worrying about money, health insurance, and the future cost of college.

My medical bills mount, even as Hillary Rodham Clinton speaks. Mary broke her arm when she fell down at school. I wasn't at home, so the school nurse called my ever-dependable brother George, who went and got her to a doctor. Result, $612 to set a child's arm. George is wonderful. He may not be there for me at the ballot box since he remains a rabid Republican, but he is there for all of us any other time. And he has to put up with eighteen hours a week on a dialysis machine because his kidneys don't function. The one time he admitted the Democrats did anything worthwhile was when Medicare took care of getting him a dialysis machine for home use. He and his wife, Jean, have made the best of that confinement, even though it means they watch more TV than Mary.

The month brought other medical bills. Tommy lost his glasses ($65 for another eye examination, and $125 for the new glasses). And the fall season ushered in Liz's allergies. While she didn't complain, she sneezed and wheezed so much, it sent us to the discount drugstore for medicine ($58 for daytime/ nighttime pills, nose spray, cough drops, and Kleenex). Funny thing about allergies. I blame the nightly weathermen for stirring them up because they tell you how much cedar pollen and mold is in the air. And all Austin starts sneezing on cue.

I don't have allergies, but while Mary was collecting autographs on her cast, I was succumbing to worry. And worries tend to run away with me. I even worry about the raccoons in my attic, a noisy bunch. Every morning when they wake me with their thumping right over my bed probably in some raccoon act of love, I worry about the electrical wires, and whether to call the animal patrol to evict them with a Havahart trap ($48). Or should I take a chance on another repair for the electrical wires ($256.79 last time around)? How can I get more speeches to pay for the upkeep of the kids? Is there enough milk in the refrigerator for tomorrow's cereal ($2.19 a gallon)?

How long could I keep this up? LBJ used to say, "Liz would charge hell with a bucket of water." But at that point, I wanted a fire hose with hydraulic pressure and a dozen relatives holding it.

Then Ed (Watch-for-My-Picture-on-the-Envelope) McMahon came into my life and offered me the solution: money! Ed McMahon and his sweepstakes would be a much better solution to my problems than a husband.

Ed first entered my life on television, and shortly afterward, in my mailbox. He had an Irish smile and seemed so friendly and sincere, just like a Boy Scout who would want to help an old lady across the street, or give her a hand in raising children. Here was my answer! I began replying to his mail like a maniac, filling out forms, double-checking the gold seal and the bonus numbers, and pasting the stickers on the magazine orders. Gluing little car-shaped stamps in the proper place so I could win the bonus Jaguar. Weeks passed and I wouldn't hear from him. After all his promises, he had only given me hope. Then another envelope would appear. But Ed was still hanging on to every one of his cotton-picking ten million dollars. Does anyone ever win the Ed McMahon contest? Or do we suckers just wind up buried at home under a stack of unwanted magazines?

Finally, there arrived the hard-core sales pitch— an envelope with my name—ELIZABETH CARPENTER—in boldface. Ed was writing to tell me that he had a truck parked down the street, just waiting to drop the money my way. To prove it, a TV ad appears with the truck unloading money for former winners who are shrieking with happiness. This could happen to me. This could happen if I subscribed to three more magazines, licked the stickers again, and placed them on the return letter where the spaces are out- lined to make it easy. So, I picked out *Time*, *News- week*, and *Boy's Life* for Tommy. I barely had it in the mailbox when in came more mail from other sweep- stakes urging me to buy jewelry in California and persimmons or some other exotic fruit in Florida. They also wanted me to make some phone calls on a 900 number at $4.98 per minute and punch the right button and maybe there was a prize awaiting me. I tried it and after ten minutes on the phone ($49.80 later) I had finally won—a coupon for $3 off my next oil change.

By the time I got the next envelope from Ed—which was a matter of minutes—I was hopelessly addicted to the wacky get-rich-quick world of chance. I sub- scribed to three more magazines—*Good Housekeep- ing*, *McCall's*, *Rolling Stone* (because Tommy was contemptuous of my selection of *Boy's Life*). Ed was no longer my only hope. For backup in case Ed didn't come through, I joined in the Reader's Digest Sweepstakes, which prompted me to buy eight books on gardening, cooking, household tips, photography (for Liz), and travel. My mailbox was beginning to jam with 900-number rip-offs that cost $6.98 for the first minute. Is it possible that Ed had squealed on me and given out my address to a lot of sweepstakes strangers?

I was peppered with new letters—offers to buy Pierre Cardin luggage, a set of books on the world of animals, monogrammed steak knives. After three months, I had more magazines coming in than most public libraries. I drew the line at *Breastfeeding* and *Cement Journal,* but *Omni, American Artist,* and *Creative Quilting* now showed up in our house. The postman complained and hinted at a cut in case I won.

Still, the letters kept coming. Each piece was carefully filed so that when the final announcement came I would have my confirmation number handy to claim the prize. I now have a file cabinet full of empty promises: 16 red Chevrolet Luminas, 12 cruises for two with mad money included, 375 deluxe audio/video entertainment centers, 1,921 color TVs with remote control, 742 VCRs, 7 video camcorders, and one astonishing multicarat genuine cubic zirconium.

I even began visualizing me and the kids in front of
TV cameras accepting the award. I would shriek,
maybe even swoon, and Tommy and Liz would prop
me up, all the while Mary and I would have our
hands tightly clutching the oversize presentation
check with my name on it.

Ed didn't let up: ELIZABETH CARPENTER has won
$1,666,675.00 Guaranteed. Payment to begin . . .
and here's the catch: I could never find the line that
said when the payment would begin. Every time he
asked how I wanted it—cash up front, yearly install-
ments, or treasury bonds?—I picked cash, in the fer-
vent hope I would still be alive when the check
arrived.

Some friends thought I had gone around the bend
with my fanatic attachment to Ed because it was
taking a lot of time. They didn't realize how much I
needed that money. Then the Texas lottery came
along. Governor Ann Richards brought it to Texas in
hopes of picking us up out of the economic dol-
drums. All this was a new scene for me, having
grown up in Texas politics when a candidate could
get elected on a three-pronged platform: paying your
honest debts, saving your seed potatoes, and being
baptized by total immersion. Ann was for all of those,
but she also wanted to build a "New Texas" with a
lottery. Between licking stamps for Ed McMahon and
the Reader's Digest Sweepstakes, I now had to pick

up lottery tickets on a regular basis and be home to check the numbers every Wednesday and Saturday nights at 9:59. I was getting worn out with get-rich schemes.

Sensing my mood, Ed, with his deep perspective powers, moved my name from the bottom of the five-person list to the top. So the next letter showed up with the bold giant letters ELIZABETH CARPENTER on top, pointed for the van of money. And in the letter, he said that he is truly glad that I am sure to win over the other four names in the final running.

Well, I missed again and I am beginning to lose faith in Ed. Not enough to stop licking and stamping and subscribing to magazines that continually litter my house, however. Maybe *Cement Journal* will come in handy after all.

While I am discouraged, I keep dreaming that I just might wind up with the prize. I know exactly how to spend the ten million. First, a health plan for all three kids. Second, pay off all the bills and establish educational trusts.

Then I'm heading to a fat farm. I'll come home thinner and younger, buy a red feather boa, and have myself a time while the kids are off at college.

9

The Bay of Pigs

$\mathcal{T}$he quality of mercy—or patience—is strained with teenagers. All of them. One minute I am sympathetic to their difficult situation and then something makes my sympathy fade into indignation and rage, like the clutter problems, or their evasion of any order to clean it up. Show me a teenage neatnik and I will give you my sweepstakes winnings!

I had forgotten how fast kids can mess up a tidy house. Despite my pleas, it never gets any better. It's not just the sneakers and boots, which are strewn from the living room through the hall to my bedroom, or the book bags. But how can anyone drop four pairs of jeans and a hairbrush on the floor without a guilty conscience?

One morning, it was especially awful here in the

Bay of Pigs—orange peelings on the bathroom sink, glasses and cups left at random. Didn't anyone pick up anything except me? What kind of people would drop grape stems on the rug, or manage to leave six, no, seven wet towels between the shower and the bedroom? People between twelve and sixteen, that's who. My blood pressure was rising and I was in for a stroke if I didn't vent my anger.

I told all three kids they needed to take a more active role in keeping the house clean. No response. They just stared at me as if I had suddenly grown three heads. I wasn't getting through.

After much prodding, Tommy finally spoke up. "But, Liz, you don't understand," he began in that tone he would use to address some dotty fool. "Having our room slightly messy makes it feel more like home."

"Yeah," Liz and Mary chimed in.

Cozy I could handle, but not a dump in a Third World country—and besides, what did they know? If they wanted to live in this house, it would take an effort on their part to keep it habitable.

While out for dinner that night, I spotted the perfect sign to post in the house:

Teenagers!
Tired of being harassed by your elders?

Act Now
**Move out, get a job, and pay your bills
while you still know everything.**

When I returned to the house, I posted the sign on
the bulletin board hoping they would see it and realize how difficult it is being around teenagers who
think they know best. They didn't find it humorous.
In fact, one of them wrote, "What's *your* problem?"

Obviously, I need better understanding of this age
group. I again called my son, Scott, to talk about my
problems, and he urged me to read Dr. Spock on the
teenage years. "Mom, the teens are a time when the
kids are trying to get out from under your wing and
you are trying to keep them there," Scott summarized.

I sent Paula, my assistant, to the public library to
bring me Dr. Spock and any other reference books
because it was getting harder and harder for me to
move around. My ankle had begun to ache so much
I could hardly stand. So she had to be my legs.

I pored over Dr. Spock. He can scare you to death.
I found myself getting more depressed as I read his
advice.

Dr. Spock's message is that the least little thing
you do or say to correct the bad habits of teenagers
may have a deep and lasting psychological impact.
And to make matters worse, each child will respond

differently to criticism, so a middle child will feel different from a first child, or a last. Spock didn't get to the ten-child family like my brother's.

I can imagine what the good doctor would say about these three kids being around someone who raises her voice because she has high expectations that they might possibly pick up their clothes, make good grades, and live a tidy and successful life. But, according to Spock, I should always have a smile at the ready, forget reprimands, and consider getting these kids to counseling—at eighty dollars a session. Otherwise, they will be permanent bed-wetters and thumb-suckers.

"Rebellion," Dr. Spock says, "is only the prelude to the more difficult problem which the youth has to face—in finding out what sort of person he wants to be as an adult. What kind of work will he want to do?"

Well, I could tell Dr. Spock a thing or two. These kids are going to be poetry-writing, well-read, foot-dragging slobs. And the only career they now qualify for is trash maker. They can make it but they don't know how to dispose of it. The backseat of my car looks like a moving slum. Right now, Tommy's beloved CD player is covered with Coke cans and pizza leftovers, along with a lot of strewn papers. Three hundred dollars' worth of stereo equipment buried in a trash heap. Am I the only one irritated by the sight of trash in my car and in my house?

I must do something short of murder about their silent indifference to neatness and order. But Dr. Spock won't let me because of the possible consequences. Why didn't he just keep marching in peace demonstrations and quit antagonizing a lot of us who are trying to make kids responsible citizens?

Paula found other books to help guide me. One was called *Talking with Teenagers*, which, the author admitted, is sometimes impossible to do since they don't talk.

Mary is at times like a silent robot, and then, if asked about a movie she has seen, she can tell you the whole plot nonstop. Liz is well read but, unlike her sister, doesn't mind sharing her experiences with adults. She amazes me with her knowledge of trivia. We'll be sitting at the dinner table eating and she can come up with the complete history of Caesar salad, which, she read somewhere, was invented in Las Vegas.

Tommy's conversation is more generous, but his mind is usually concentrating on his girlfriends. Amazingly, at the moment, all their first names begin with L: Lydia, Laura, and Lisa. Maybe this helps keep them straight for him. Maybe he is moving through the alphabet, because last month there was Katy, Katherine, and Kim.

I have learned, however, how to grab him for a conversation. Hand him something to eat that he likes—

say, mini-pizzas or chicken nuggets. Point to a chair
(try to refrain from saying "Heel"). And he may sit
down a minute and talk, preferably on American Indian rituals, or the birth of the blues. Unfortunately,
I don't even know how to lead him into a conversation on either subject. And this depresses me a lot
because I am dying to talk with these kids about
something besides homework and dinner.

Again my old reporting instincts gnaw at me. I
want to know what is going on in their young minds
in the nineties.

It really is tough and I can't seem to make it easier.
I worry . . . God, how I worry . . . not only about a
sloppy house but also about sloppy homework, getting groceries and paying for them. The more I worry
the more I find myself, normally a healthy, hearty
woman, feeling age encroaching on my energies.

Like Lyndon Johnson, I want everything to be done
yesterday. When it wasn't, LBJ was likely to pick you
up by the ears as he did his beagles. The kids—with
all ears intact—have perfected "the stall." They pro-
crastinate, put off, forget, lose, or simply play deaf to
my request.

"Hold on" is Mary's favorite way of putting something off. She'd probably have you "hold on" if you
were in the middle of a heart attack. Tommy plays
deaf and I wonder if perhaps he really is. Shouting or
throwing your body in front of him is the only way to

grab his attention (unless you're waving food under his nose).

I decided to hold a powwow over dinner to address "the stall." Everyone would make two lists: a list of things they automatically stall, and another list of things they would never put off for a minute. When Liz, Tommy, and Mary came to the dinner table, I made a game of the lists.

"First off, everybody, what do teenagers like to delay?" I asked.

They stalled, typically, but then we had a staccato of:

"Homework!"

"Setting the table."

"Taking out trash."

Each one was talking about the sins of the other.

Tommy flinched with mention of the trash because he is guilty of ignoring it over and over each Monday and Thursday when the trash truck arrives before eight A.M. I've tried everything to prod his memory—signs on the fridge, which seem clear enough to me—TOMMY, TAKE OUT THE TRASH TODAY. Once, I even bundled the trash bags and put them in front of the door so he couldn't miss them. So what did he do? He carefully set them aside and headed off to school.

Liz looked sheepish when she pointed out another stalling vice.

"Returning library books," she said.

Both Liz and Mary have such a bad record at the public library that Liz once had to take out a new card under an assumed name and use a friend's address.

"Sending thank-you notes!" I injected. Last Christmas, under supervision, Mary and Liz wrote all their thank-you notes for gifts received. I stamped them and gave them to Liz to mail. She stuck them in her purse. That was early January.

Six months later—in June—I found them in the same purse, now unused. I sent them anyway to startled friends who could barely remember giving the gift.

"Taking a shower," Tommy suggested. "I can put that off without even thinking about it."

"Finishing a shower," I said, alluding to the fact that Liz can go through thirty-five gallons of water before quitting.

"Deciding what to eat," Tommy said, though this is not his flaw. He can decide in a New York minute. "Mary can stand in front of the icebox with both doors flung open staring like it's a TV set."

He's right. Once I interrupted her, "Why are you staring into the refrigerator?" I asked.

"I don't know," she replied.

"Maybe you are hungry?" I nudged.

"Not really."

"Well, watch out for frostbite!" I warned.

In contrast, Tommy is decisive about food. He opens the door of the fridge and in a blink of an eye has a sandwich in one hand and a carton of milk in the other.

By now, because the list was growing and they enjoyed getting at each other, we tried the second question.

"What do teenagers never forget to do?"

"Hang out at the mall with friends," Mary replied.

"Malls are *so* dorky, Mary," Liz said. "Only babies hang out there. Get a life."

"I have one," Mary retorted.

Before this escalated into the next world war, I put up my hands and called "Whoa! What else do teenagers think is important?"

"Their birthday when they will get a car," Tommy piped up. I was aware that Tommy had been thinking about cars since he was fourteen, and time was marching on.

If he would only spend the same amount of brain energy on school that he does researching the classified ads for a car, he would be the Einstein of his generation.

10

Et Tu, Little Caesar's?

*T*hree hungry appetites sent me to the grocery store almost daily. I think I spent more time there than the manager.

Tommy said he'd gladly take over this task when he could drive, and I was getting as eager as he was for that to happen. Sixteen is the legal driving age in Texas, but you can get a license earlier if you can prove your family has a hardship. I thought I had lots of them, but my bad ankle and advancing age were all we'd need to qualify Tommy for the special license. I was counting down the minutes.

Meanwhile, I was becoming less picky about old-fashioned nutritious meals.

Kids are omnivorous, but they like it plain. So forget the caviar. Put away the oyster forks. Throw out the Charlotte russe pan. These kids will eat anything. They can go through a bowl of grapes faster than Caesar Chavez could have picked them. At this house, we don't know what leftovers are!

When school is out, danger! I used to think of this hour as "snack time." Those words are too gentle. If the breakfast counter doesn't have anything edible on it, they will eat the breakfast counter. Raging hunger is a common trait.

And beware if dinner is cooked and waiting on the stove. More than once I have thrown my body in front of it in a spread-eagle position to save it for later. One Easter Sunday I had prepared dinner for friends who were coming back from church service with me. I came home with them to find the roast cleaned to the bone. Tommy had eaten it all for breakfast.

Why is it this came as a shock to me? Because when I was raising my own two teenagers, I had a cook, a marvelous North Carolina woman named Ruth. Where is Ruth now that I really need her? Well, she's working at a bank where "I have my own desk," she told me proudly when I called her long distance. So the cooking for these three hungry teenagers fell on me, and it cost five times more than the grocery bill for one widow.

One hunger rush prompted me to remember a time long ago on a safari to Africa when I watched the mother lions kill a wildebeest and leave it a few moments so the male lions could come in for the best parts. When the Kings of the Jungle had done their damage, the docile lionesses returned for the bones. There at my home on Skyline Drive, the "Kings of the Jungle" were Tommy and his friends—all fourteen- to sixteen-year-old males. You could almost hear them roar "FOOD!" at the icebox door.

I don't mean to make light of the problems of Bosnia, but the United Nations should know that I could use an airlift of edibles too.

I've always loved to cook, but my repertoire had really shrunk over the years. I'd forgotten how hard it is to come up with something different for dinner night after night. Liz, Tommy, and Mary weren't ex- actly picky eaters—Lord knows these are kids who'd eat meatloaf for breakfast and think Chef Boyardee really owns a restaurant somewhere—but I felt obliged to try to vary what I put on the table. How many nights in a row can Perdue *do* it? Plus I was going broke buying Chinese take-out. Something had to give.

So I consulted the nearest food experts, my sister- in-law Jean, who is a home economics professor, and a good friend, Anita Davis, who is the Julia Child of Westlake Hills. Anita can be seen on most any special day—Ash Wednesday, Shrove Tuesday, Groundhog Day—bearing cakes and cookies to some class at school.

I presented my problem to both experts: how to fill

up the bottomless pits and remain solvent at the bank. Jean was more help on the solvency problem. She weathered the Great Depression by scraping bowls so clean they didn't have to be washed. She has been known to wrap a few bread crumbs in cellophane to be used for some future meatloaf. Jean offered to shop for me at Sam's, the big discount grocery store inconveniently located twenty miles across town, where you can buy large quantities at discount.

When it comes to food, Anita is more reckless. She is the only person I know who buys chocolate chips by the ten-pound bag. Her giant cookie jar is never empty. And what is really disgusting is that her husband, Ron, and her daughter, Katherine, magically remain thin.

Anita informed me she also had a card to shop at Sam's and would tote food in from the bargain boondocks for me at any given hour. As time went by, Tommy and Mary and Liz grew taller and taller and hungrier and hungrier. My ankle had grown a lot weaker since the kids arrived, and I could no longer navigate the fifteen-lane supermarket near my house. Pretty soon it took both Jean and Anita to fill my grocery list. I accepted more speech invitations to pay for the tab, including one from the American Association of Retired People, which upped my fee when I explained my situation.

I needed to think of good tasty foods that wouldn't break the bank and that wouldn't take forever to fix. Anita, who was once an executive planner for a food chain, decided to go about solving my problem systematically. She thought a food-tasting party would be fun. She would prepare several Teenager Specials that were interesting, not overly complicated, and best of all, that wouldn't cost a fortune. I would supply ten teenagers to test and grade them.

I arrived at her house with Tommy and Mary and eight teenage friends at the hungry hour—five-thirty P.M.—the same hour, incidentally, as national network news, from which I have now been cut off for three years. Has the Gulf War ended yet?

Anita was ready. A picturesque smorgasbord lay before us. This table didn't just groan. It screamed.

Pigs in blankets, carrot sticks, and three kinds of dips, Anita's Super Lasagne oozing with hot melted cheese, a big platter of chicken rolled and baked with a crushed cornflake crust, a plate of pita pockets, and a baked potato bar with all the fixin's—butter, sour cream, bacon bits, and cheese toppings. These potatoes were grown for mature sizes only.

All this was just for starters. The smorgasbord lopped over onto the sideboard for desserts. There was a giant plate of pancake-size cookies with smiling faces on them in raisins and red hots, then an assorted plate of three of her best cookie recipes: a hand-size sugar cookie shaped like the map of Texas with raisins marking the major cities, chewy brownies, and—yes—the family favorite, chocolate chip cookies. She informed us there was plenty of ice cream in assorted flavors in the freezer if anyone wanted it. The evening had grown from a taste test to a feast. But what the heck? It all worked great, and the kids' eyes grew wide when they saw the spread. Forget about the way to a man's heart. Food is for getting to teenagers.

The kids were like racehorses straining at the gate as I said a hurried blessing: "Thank you, God, for a bounty that only You and Anita could cook up."

And then we were into it! For twenty-five minutes conversation was at a standstill. The only sound was munching and crunching. The piles of food began to disappear. Anita had set up the array to be eaten chronologically—snacks, entrées, and desserts—but order was a victim of the stampede.

Mary was already trying to stretch one giant bite of Texas cookie—from Corpus Christi to Amarillo—into her mouth, and Tommy and friends were inhaling the chicken and lasagne.

Finally, though, they were full. Anita smiled in happy satisfaction and handed out plastic baggies to take home leftovers.

But not before we polled the group for favorites. And the winners? The do-it-yourself potato bar was first by a landslide. Anita's Super Lasagne came in second, and George Bush's Broccoli, third.

First Prize: Potato Bar

Select two large potatoes for each guest (one apiece if the guests aren't teens).

Scrub clean, grease, and make holes with fork.

Bake in 350-degree oven for one full hour or until a fork slides in easily.

Slice each potato open four ways and arrange on platter.

Prepare bowls of sour cream, bacon bits, butter, chives, salt and pepper to taste.

Place all these on a counter or bar. Let them have at it.

Second Prize: Super Lasagne

1 box (8 ozs.) lasagne noodles
¾ lb. ground beef
¾ lb. medium-hot sausage meat
1 jar (30 ozs.) spaghetti sauce
2 eggs
1 carton (16 ozs.) cottage cheese
16 ozs. mozzarella cheese, shredded
2 tbsps. minced parsley, fresh or dried

Cook lasagne noodles. After draining the noodles cover with cold water to keep them from sticking together. Meanwhile, crumble and brown the ground beef and sausage, stirring and separating with a fork. Drain off fat. Add sauce, stir, and set aside.

In a separate bowl, mix eggs, cottage cheese, mozzarella (reserving ½ cup for topping), and parsley.

Coat the bottom of a 12 × 8-inch baking dish with sauce mixture. Layer lasagne noodles, ⅓ of the sauce, and ½ of the cheese mixture. Repeat. Top with noodles, the remainder of the sauce, and the reserved ½ cup of mozzarella.

Bake in a 350-degree oven for one hour. Let sit for 10–15 minutes before cutting in squares and serving.

If there are leftovers, wrap individual portions in plastic wrap, freeze, and pop in the microwave for single servings.

Third Prize: Broccoli Fit for George Bush (who never liked the stuff)

Steam fresh or frozen broccoli parts. Make a white sauce with sherry and add almond slivers. Or you can mix Dijon mustard and plain yogurt for a tasty, healthful alternative.

My contribution to the testing and tasting party were educational fortune cookies. Mary and Liz both love Chinese food and think the fortune cookies should guide them through life. I came up with a way to convey my messages and not be accused of preaching. I bought fortune cookies and with tweezers slipped out the store-bought fortunes and inserted some of my own with tiny handprinted messages. This requires patience and a Machiavellian mind. Here are some of my favorites:

He who wears dirty T-shirt must use Chinese laundry.
Homework begun gets done.
He who speeds pays for costly deeds.
Periods of household improvement are in your future.
Too little work causes Looney Teens.
He who washes plate will be rewarded.
Too much hard rock leads to early deafness.

The possibilities are endless, particularly if you compose these after downing two glasses of champagne. Once this prompted me to write: "Sex gives acne!"

Tommy added one other:

"Confucius say: 'He who lies with the women forget not his condom-ents.' "

11

Tom Thumb
and the BMW Blues

$\mathcal{M}$y life with teenagers and cars covered months of getting them legally licensed and several arrests after that. Today I am a much wiser woman. What have I learned? I have learned there is one thing thirstier than Dean Martin, and that's the vintage BMW that I bought for Tommy. This BMW was old as Methuselah, had run more miles than Jesse Owens, and still managed to look as distinguished as Alistair Cooke.

It only cost $3,222. At first! But that was only the beginning. It was always in need of oil, water, air, steering fluid, brake fluid, gas, gas, gas. It would have been cheaper to run it on straight gin.

The entire epic of helping two teenagers obtain a car conjures up a series of drama-filled flashbacks.

Mostly the action focuses on Tommy more than

Liz, even though they got their licenses together. By the time he reached his fifteenth birthday, Tommy was chomping at the bit for a car. And so was I, present unpaid chauffeur of all three kids. In Texas, as I mentioned, you can get a driver's license at fifteen if you can prove it is needed to relieve a hardship at home. I was, of course, the hardship—aging aunt with rampant arthritis.

There were some limitations to the license; most important, he wasn't allowed to drive alone after sundown. But it was essential that Tommy be able to help out with the driving. The chauffeuring duties were killing me: waking the kids at seven A.M., knowing they would snooze until seven-thirty. Then, stuffing breakfast into them, reminding them of schoolbags, glasses, and lunch money, and getting them into my car by eight A.M., where they quickly turned on the worst music ever composed.

Then, running the errands to the grocery store and cleaners and back by three-thirty P.M. to pick them up at school. There was always a soccer practice or a music lesson or a visit to a friend's house. Tommy's piano teacher, a nineteen-year-old Chinese student named Lei Laing, had to be picked up, brought to my house for an hour's lesson once a week, and then driven back to his apartment house. He may have faced the tanks at Tiananmen Square, but he didn't know how to drive.

Weekends were full of uncertainty and sleeplessness. I was driving all three kids to school dances across town or to the movies at nine-thirty or ten o'clock on Friday and Saturday, when they might get around to making up their mind about what they were going to do. I saw a lot of *Saturday Night Live* on TV while trying to stay awake to pick them up afterward. Was this my destiny? I felt like jumping off the Congress Avenue bridge, but it would be my luck to survive, or to land on my bad ankle. If Tommy and Liz learned to drive, I reasoned, I could be relieved of all this weekend misery.

The first step was to pass driver's school and get a license. While we shopped for a car for Tommy, I enrolled both Liz and Tommy with a driving instructor. Fortunately, I didn't have to worry about a vehicle for Liz. Her mother, Nancy, offered an aged but operational blue truck Liz could use, and Liz thought it was "really cool" to drive a wreck to a fancy private school. Tommy visualized a Great Gatsby–type car. A single car for both to share was impossible because Liz was now in the private school across town, ten miles to the east, and Tommy and Mary were four miles to the west.

I picked the wrong driving instructor. He did most of his instruction in a late-afternoon special class working from a blackboard. This was dull stuff to these kids, who were lurching to get on the road.

When he finally took the students out for test driving, it was in his 1968 Chevrolet Impala, about the size of the *Titanic*. Fortunately there was a passenger brake pedal so the instructor could control the car if necessary. This was frequently necessary!

The kids wanted to practice driving with me every time they got the chance. If I needed to run an errand, one of them would say, "Do you need me to drive you?"

I always replied with a quick, "Not today."

One day after being harassed far too many times, I capitulated. Liz could drive me to and from the grocery store. We set out.

I was terrorized, clinging to the door as though I were going to abandon ship.

"Watch it!" I shrieked over and over. "Did you see that deer . . . that truck . . . that house?"

"You know," Liz said in an indulgent voice, "my instructor doesn't have a problem with my driving. In fact, he must find it very relaxing, because he always falls asleep."

I couldn't tell her the truth. I'm sure it was his only coping mechanism left.

Texas, a place of wide-open spaces and high-risk habits, doesn't require that kids pass a driving test. All that has to be done is to certify that they have driven a car for eight hours. This entitles them to a full driver's license, which is one reason we find so many dead armadillos in the roads. We even have a car cemetery somewhere out in Amarillo for the Cadillacs that have died. Probably at the hands of teenage drivers.

In six weeks, both kids passed their driving courses. They were now legally licensed. Liz got her truck with its questionable life expectancy and Tommy was churning to buy the promised car. We set out to agree on one that I could afford and Tommy liked.

We must have tracked classified ads to at least twenty-five used-car lots, which led us to even more used-car salesmen. Used-car salesmen have been given a bad name—at least two of the ones we encountered warned me that the car Tommy wanted wouldn't make it around the block.

Tommy would have driven out with any number of the BMWs or Mercedeses we saw. He particularly liked a Karmann-Ghia. I had never heard that name before and when I did, I assumed it was some Mafia don.

We had different standards for a car. Tommy's first priority was that it have personality. He had seen too many old movies, because he was into old classic-looking cars with a certain atmosphere.

My priority was that it run, and have a certain guarantee that it would continue to run.

Finally we spotted one that seemed to qualify for

both of us: a maroon BMW, which had been driven 110,000 miles in its eleven-year history. What cinched it for me was the fact that the used-car man gave me a warranty for six months. What cinched it for Tommy was it looked distinguished and had a stereo. It did not have power steering, which eliminated me and my arthritic hands as a driver.

But I wasn't born yesterday—in fact, it was several days before yesterday. I took time to draw up a contract for Tommy to sign upon receiving it—a contract carefully setting forth his duties for the privilege of using the car. When the call came that the car was ready, Paula, and my young assistant, and I were eager to surprise Tommy at school.

We went to Tommy's school to make the presentation. In hand was the agreement and a camera to record the day the long-awaited BMW came into our lives. The school bell rang. Tommy emerged and suddenly spied us. A big smile spread all over his face and he ran over to us. He circled the car, checking it all out. Clearly this almost religious experience was a rite of passage. I put the contract on the fender of the car with a pen and he readily signed the agreement without even reading it. I would make sure he did later.

To: Tommy, who this day becomes chairman of the transportation committee for Liz Carpenter, be-

loved and trusting aunt of beloved and trustworthy nephew.

Because we believe this can be the happiest day of your life, your passage into reliable almost-man-hood, we offer with loving heart these guidelines.

1. Above all, be careful of others' lives and your own life. You mean a lot to our family.

2. Choose safety over risk.

3. You are charged with delivering and returning your younger sister, Mary Sutherland, delightful so-cially active teenager, to and from school daily; also to various activities when possible. These duties will be shared by others.

4. You will be purchasing agent for groceries for this household, learning comparative shopping habits as you proceed to pick them up and deliver to kitchen and possibly icebox. You will do this at least twice a week.

Signed this 2nd of November in the year of the Dem-ocrats, 1992

_____   _____

Tommy Sutherland, Nephew   Liz Carpenter, Aunt

I also had a letter for him to carry in his wallet, in case he got stopped driving in times other than those authorized for hardship licenses.

This is to state that my nephew, Tommy Suther-land, is primarily undertaking delivery tasks for

*me, such as grocery shopping, delivering, and
whatever is needed to make my life, as an elderly
and infirm woman, possible.*

What a relief for me the first time I heard the car
drive up at four P.M. after school. Free! Free at last!
Tommy had Mary in the front seat and they were
both rocking to Pearl Jam. Best of all, I did not have
to leave my computer at three-fifteen and battle the
younger, more agile afternoon mothers picking up
their school kids.

I had to get insurance on a fifteen-year-old male
driver before I let him take the wheel, and I couldn't
believe that it cost two thousand dollars a year to
keep him insured! It turns out the track record of
teenage boy drivers is abysmal. (Why am I surprised?) They average three tickets in the first six
months for violations and possible damage.

Within three months, Tommy had barely missed
the averages. He had two altercations with the police, which required two different court appearances,
luckily in different courts, so I only had to be humiliated once with each of them. The first court date was
at the crowded Austin traffic violations department.
This was for running into the back of a car because
he was playing with the radio while taking his sister
to school. The Austin police lady "was real nice,"
Tommy reported. She said she liked his brown eyes.

So since there wasn't any real damage she didn't charge him with hitting another car, only with forgetting his driver's license. When we produced the driver's license in the traffic violations department, they dropped charges. Tommy smiled, relieved he didn't have to go to the electric chair. (I had warned him about this.)

But on ticket number two, a few weeks later, the male cop didn't care a whit about Tommy's eyes—so when he failed to stop at the new stop sign about a block from our house, and it was midnight and he was unaccompanied by an adult, the police officer stuck him with three violations:

1) Not having his insurance in the front compartment. That's a law in Texas that is probably good, but I have always thought it showed the state was in cahoots with the insurance companies.

2) Driving alone with a hardship license at midnight.

3) Failure to stop at a stop sign.

We reported to the West Lake courtroom on the given day, and it was old home week for Tommy. This was a juvenile court, and about thirty kids from the neighborhood and Westlake High School were there on various traffic offenses.

The circuit-riding judge saw them one by one and

I hobbled in with Tommy—my walking cane in full view for sympathy. The judge wasn't all that moved. He lectured Tommy, for which I was glad, and then stuck me with a fifty-eight-dollar fine, which he said Tommy should pay off by working. That was fine with me, but I wish the judge had come along to oversee it. Then he added probation for 180 days and a requirement he take eight hours of defensive driving. Another eighteen dollars for me.

There was one more altercation within the month. In getting out of a parking space, Tommy scraped the side of a young lady's new sports car.

"I gave her your insurance company's number, and she was very nice about it and didn't call the police," Tommy reported.

How did he manage to bump into so many kindly people?

When the police tickets slowed down, the repair bills speeded up. Everything went wrong with the BMW. All of it conveniently after the six-month warranty had expired, of course. It needed new tires— four of them. It needed new brakes. The oil system was totally out of whack and Tommy didn't know why the red light kept flashing to tell him to FILL UP WITH OIL. He ignored it and pretty soon the BMW simply gave up, and so we had to buy a new engine. Already, I was three thousand dollars into repairs on a car that cost three thousand two hundred and twenty dollars. Obviously I was playing a losing game. Then a wild idea came to me! Instead of buying Tommy a new car that would run, why didn't I let him use my reliable car, and I would buy myself a new car. Everyone is always telling me to be good to myself, and here was my chance.

I have this habit of following up on fast decisions before I change my mind or, worse still, forget. I didn't even want to leave the comfort of my couch. If QVC sold cars I suppose I would have ordered one up along with some of Carol Channing's diamond jewelry. But they don't, so I called a friendly Texas Ford dealer and told them I wanted the best riding car they had at the least expensive price—and reminded them I was a senior citizen. (I've learned to toss that in because sometimes it wins a discount.)

Done! Next day, without even picking the color, I had my phone-order car, a shiny new twilight-blue four-door sedan at as good a price as I could get with Henry Ford's rebates. Tommy had a car that would work. And, best of all, someone else had the BMW. I went to bed smiling.

12

⟪∞⟫

Thirteen!

*M*ary turned thirteen. Thirteen is the worst age going. When people are asked what age they would like to be, they say twenty-one or thirty-nine. No one says thirteen! It is a problem-ridden time full of the growing pains between childhood and adolescence, of testing your limits and your parents.

I remember little about my own thirteenth year, although I do have a reminder, this classic letter my brother Tom wrote me on my birthday:

September 1, 1933

Dear Mary Elizabeth,
    Congratulations on having gotten into your teens. Thirteen is about the swellest age to be in

and has twice as much excitement as the rest of your life put together. Of course, the rest of your life is put together anyway. I say put together because a girl doesn't have to do anything but entertain herself. A boy has to worry about what he's going to be—not that he'll ever be anything, but he has to decide and make up his mind and answer people's questions about it until he hardly has time to do anything exciting enough to get whipped for.

With girls it's different. They get away with anything; that's the nice part of being a girl. Girls don't have to worry about anything because they know that all they have to do is grow up and then some boy falls in love with them and marries them and makes them a living so that they never have to do anything, only have babies as fast as she can.

And girls while they are growing up have nothing at all to do or think about except have fun from morning to night. They don't have to be good, like boys, because people just take it for granted that they are good and never want any proof. When a girl wants something people won't give her, all she has to do is jump up and down and chew the bed clothes and cry and people just have to give her what she wants right away to stop her, because you can't hit her over the head like you can a boy. And besides, boys aren't smart enough to think of such a way of getting what they want. Girls are smart, and no matter what they do, even to using their big sister's smelly perfume, they can lie out of it just as easy as falling off a calf.

Happy Birthday!

My love to all, and especially to Mama because

she's the kind of mama who sends me $10 instead of $5.

                                        Tom

That says a lot about Tom. Of course, he meant it whimsically, I think, but it is his babies I am now raising and I can't help but grimace at how lackadaisically he assumed women take care of the kids.

Every twelve-year-old dreams of finally being a teenager, and Mary was no exception. I told her she could have a few friends—all girls—over for the great event. By *few* I thought four or five, but a dozen prepubescent girls showed up.

It would turn out to be the night Mary met her first police officer eyeball to eyeball. I should have realized it was an omen.

For hours on end, it seemed, the house was full of teenagers screaming and squealing when anyone mentioned a boy's name. The bum-de-bum music never stopped. Every song seemed to rock the neighborhood. The neighbors must have agreed, for the militia arrived. The stereo went off.

Later, around midnight, one of Mary's friends came to me and said that the pizza was here and she needed twenty-five dollars to pay for it. *Pizza!* After feeding them a tray of cold cuts, two loaves of bread, twenty-four mini-pizzas, four bags of nachos, two jugs of queso, six packets of Oreo cookies, forty-eight mini-muffins, a pound of M&M's, a large rectangle sheet cake, and two quarts of ice cream—they ordered pizza. No way was I paying for that one. The pizza delivery boy looked dejected, but I stood my ground and refused to accept it.

It was past two A.M. when the girls settled. Some of them camped out in the guest house, some in Mary's bed, and most on the floor of the living room. The party was a nightmare from beginning to end. Nothing quite compares to a food fight with Oreo cookies on blue satin chairs or a can of soda being dumped into the Jacuzzi. Caesar's divide-and-conquer theory was the rule. They came, they saw, and I was exhausted.

The next day Mary said she was sorry about messing up the house. She promised it would never happen again. She even cried, a trick she had learned by being the youngest. I forgave and took her at her word.

But strange things continued to happen with this angelic-looking child, now officially a teenager. Mary started sitting for hours in front of a mirror, just staring at her reflection. I noticed an unusual shimmer on her lips—bold bronze—which made her look like an entry in the Nefertiti look-alike contest.

Her clothes were becoming monochromatic. Even on the coldest days, she wore shorts, a U2 black T-shirt screaming ACHTUNG, BABY (Danger!) and Doc

Marten boots. I always thought Doc Marten was a cough medicine, but Doc came up with a heavy designer boot that was inspired by Nazi stormtroopers. She'd bought the boots at a place called Atomic City. I got stuck with the bill for $110.

When I looked at the fashions of her friends, they all wore the same thing: stringy faded-denim shorts, the Hitler boots, and a faded T-shirt, hopefully with a clean message.

I should have been more foresighted and figured out that Mary began feeling left behind after Liz and Tommy got their driver's licenses and were away a lot more with their friends. Finally this dawned on me, so I tried to be tolerant of Mary, especially of her having friends to sleep over. One Saturday night, Tommy was away for the weekend and a friend whom I will call Jessica was spending the night with Mary.

About ten-thirty, I assumed they would soon be asleep, so I went to bed.

My phone rang at one-thirty A.M. It was the downtown Austin Police Headquarters relaying a message from a police car officer to me. He had stopped "two little girls named Mary and Jessica because they were driving the wrong way on a one-way street." And here's the ringer: the police officer said they were driving a blue Ford. My car!

What should he do?

"Wait for me. I'll be there in ten minutes," I told the

dispatcher. I bolted out of bed and roused Liz. Fortunately, her truck had gas, and she mustered enough energy to get us there while I hung on to the passenger door, which didn't quite shut.

In ten minutes we were in sight of a police car flashing its lights, and as we pulled up beside it, two very frightened little girls were clinging to each other, and Jessica was crying. To my amazement the policeman didn't give them a ticket, even though Jessica, the driver, was fourteen and obviously didn't have a license. I thanked him and got in my car to drive it home, trying to harness my anger and fear.

"Whatever possessed you?" I demanded in an icy tone.

"It was my idea," Mary whimpered.

"I'm so sorry," Jessica said between tears.

"I ought to take you right now to your parents," I answered.

"Please, please don't do that," Jessica said. "They'll hit me."

Hoping she was lying but not being really sure, I decided it was too far to take her home anyway, so I drove back to my house in cold silence. When we got there, I said as firmly as possible, "Get to your beds and I want the lights off in five minutes. We'll talk in the morning."

Next morning, two wan little girls came in and said, "We want to talk to you. We are so sorry."

"I want you both to sit here and write down all of the things that could have happened to you," I said, handing them both pencils and paper.

And they did. While still angry, I was happily surprised with the result.

Between the two they came up with some good points. Things like: "It was wrong because the car wasn't ours." "We could have had a wreck." "We could have had big fines." "We could have killed someone." "Neither of us had a license." I felt Jessica understood me best. She wrote, "I'm sorry, Liz. We betrayed you and you probably will never trust me again."

They seemed to have thought it through. "Maybe I am getting better at this kind of thing," I thought.

We were barely into thirteen and already I was discovering that it would take Sherlock Holmes, Nancy Drew, Jessica Fletcher, and three Jungian psychologists to tell you why a thirteen-year-old *has* to break rules. They're either sneaking a smoke, commandeering your car, or slipping out of the house after midnight to rendezvous with other thirteen-year-olds.

Only two weeks after Mary's Great Auto Caper, as my friends called the incident, it was the dreaded Saturday night once more. A ringing phone. I was again bolted into consciousness. I looked at the clock—thank God for lighted dials and larger digital numbers; this was getting to be a regular occurrence. It was one-thirty in the morning.

I picked up the phone.

"This is the West Lake Police and there are four little girls down at Ninety-six West Lake Drive. Does Mary Sutherland belong in your house?"

"God, yes! I thought she was sleeping in the next room," I replied.

"No, the patrol car found her and the other girls out walking along the main road. This is dangerous," said the police lady on the phone, "and we feel their parents should be called."

"It will only take me a few minutes to get there," I replied, fumbling for my bedroom slippers and a housecoat. I should start sleeping fully clothed.

I was there in five minutes. Before me were the flashing lights of three police cars, a huddle of officers, and five thirteen-year-olds, looking sheepish and disgusted that they were caught.

"We just wanted to sit outside and talk," they said from the curb in front of the Stop and Go.

"If you want to sit outside and just talk after midnight, what's wrong with my front yard, which has table, chairs, and is in reach of an icebox full of food?" No answer. I delivered them home.

Someone mumbled some kind of thank-you for taking them home, and Mary remained uncommunicative.

Soon the police lady called to see if everything was all right. She was sympathetic and had a suggestion.

"I had two girls who were like that when they were in their teens, and I cured them by taking them down to the emergency room at the hospital at one A.M. on Saturday night to show them the stabbings and victims of rape and robbery," she offered.

I'm not good with blood and broken bones or I would have been a crime reporter instead of a political journalist, so I dismissed this cure for my ailment. I hoped against all of the evidence that Mary was truly sorry and would decide to act like an adult. But I should have known better . . . and I probably should have taken her on that field trip to the E.R.

Mary did act like an adult for a few days, but the next Saturday night all pretense failed! She was to go to Karen's, and I would pick her up when I got home from a dinner party about ten-thirty or eleven P.M. But when I got home there was a message on the telephone machine. She would spend the night at another friend's, whom I'll call Brenda, the third member of this worrisome triumvirate of thirteen-year-olds.

I called Brenda's. No Mary, and worse than that, Brenda had come home, her mother said, and smelled of vodka and was in a deep sleep in bed. Called Karen. No Mary! She had left some time ago. She didn't know whether Brenda was with her or not.

Back to Brenda's mother. She had already awakened Brenda for any clues. Brenda had no memory of where Mary went. Were they protecting Mary with this loss of memory? Back to Karen on the phone. "Where did the vodka come from?" Finally, Karen, who would never outdo George Washington in a truth contest, reported that Mary had brought a bottle of vodka from my house!!! Did I even own a bottle of vodka? I made a mental note to myself to clear out the liquor cabinet the next day.

I began to panic. I got Karen's mother on the phone. Would she check the hammock in the yard, and any other places where Mary might have fallen asleep? She did—no Mary. It was approaching midnight and dark as pitch outside in this bucolic neighborhood, which has few streetlights and no sidewalks.

I kept calling Karen. Her phone was busy for forty-five minutes. Who was she alerting? My mind went wild. Yes, there was someone named Keith, a high-school student (danger!), and I dragged out of her that he lived nearby. No, she didn't know a last name but she had already phoned his house, because she did know his phone number. What is this country coming to, where kids know a phone number and no last name? Mary had been there but had left.

That was a mile from my house, and it was now nearing one in the morning. I called the West Lake

Police and the same police lady was on the phone. We were becoming weekend friends, joined by that common denominator: worry. Her familiar voice was comforting: "I'll alert the patrol cars to be on the lookout for a teenager with long blond hair. You stay by the phone in case she calls."

I was yearning to get in my car and make the rounds of the fast-food joints at the shopping center—Popeye's, where they often went, and Taco Bell. Suppose Mary had tested the vodka—and I presume that if it was my vodka, she certainly had. (Not another drop of whiskey comes in this house, I told myself . . . even though I began to sense how much I would need it.)

Meanwhile, I called Paula, who sprang out of sleep. "I'll be there in a few minutes," Paula said. And she was, arriving just after Tommy and two hungry friends had hit home and the fridge. He seemed unconcerned, but my own panic was growing along with my imagination. Taco Bell had closed. Popeye's was closed. Where had Mary passed out? My scouting team headed for the shopping center and the only two stores open: the all-night grocery stores. Paula assured me, "I'll call in twenty minutes."

Tommy and friends continued to empty the fridge, and I was increasingly indignant at their lack of concern.

"It's just a phase," he kept saying, and couldn't

seem to understand that the "phase" had a new twist tonight.

"Go check out the guest house again," I ordered Tommy. I had done this half an hour earlier. It seemed to take him forever. Finally, he brought in a very worn-out-looking Mary, still in shorts, no shoes, face strained. I demanded explanations. I got few. She had walked home from Karen's and been home for twenty minutes.

Twenty minutes! Why hadn't she checked in? She was bound to know I was frantically hunting her through the teenage network. I stormed, and sent her to bed, but only after she stopped by the fridge because "I am hungry." It was now one forty-five A.M. Paula called in and I gave her the news and felt awful that I had roused her out of bed for a midnight posse to locate Mary. "Get on the phone," I called to Mary, "and apologize to Paula."

She did, rather gracefully, as I listened in. Paula was good at the response. "Do you realize how many people are concerned about you, Mary? I have been through every Tom Thumb and Apple Tree asking the clerks if they have seen you." Mary was "sorry, really sorry," she said between bites of the sandwich.

Finally, back to bed, to toss and turn during a restless night! What was I to do? I took an extra blood pressure pill because I could feel a lot of strange pains in the base of my neck, a forerunner—I told myself—of the strokes some of my septuagenarian friends were having.

Why were these kids, who had now been with me for one year and nine months, putting me through this personal hell? Next morning, the blood pressure still didn't feel down, judging by my head, and I started composing memos to go on the bulletin board, really mean memos.

Throughout the day hurt and anger grew. I summoned my sister-in-law, Jean—a steady and firm voice. My brother George, who is recovering from a mild stroke and walks shakily with a cane, said he wanted to come too. Those two have been the rock of the family, the common sense. They've also provided the most loving voices, always there for any of us who are troubled. They came. They sat with Mary and talked, talked, talked to get at the core of what was eating at her. Was she rebelling because all thirteen-ers around the world get some sort of ESP message to "give 'em hell"? Mary wouldn't loosen up, but she listened, cried a little, and retreated to her CDs.

I slept some, and then called Molly Wing, an understanding masseuse who, even on Sunday, would put me on her clean, comfortable massage table and help me relax—which I wasn't doing yet. God knows I needed her help in my throbbing anger at the realization that I was spending the last years of my life trapped by inconsiderate teenagers.

Molly's massage room is in her home, a spacious bungalow set in an English-like garden (she and her gentle eighty-year-old mother, Kathleen, are British).

"Come on over," she said. She would shower up and get the dirt off her hands from an afternoon of gardening. There was a soft spring breeze blowing the fragrances of the garden through the massage room as I lay on the table awaiting Molly's magic hands. The birds were the only noise, but there must have been twenty kinds, judging by the contrasting bird sounds that began lulling my blood pressure down as I lay there with eyes closed. I was asleep before Molly got to me. In an hour, I had been rocked and the muscles stretched out, knots in my back gone. I began to come down from the pinnacle of indignation and think through my problem.

Should I have gotten upset? Should I have just assumed as Tommy advised that this was a phase and would one day be over? But when?

There were a number of calls on Sunday as news spread through the neighborhood of Mary's escapade and how upset I had been.

One of the callers was Mary's school counselor, who found me after the mothers' network alerted her. She had some names of private counselors in case Mary would respond to an "outside, impersonal

adult." These solid suggestions of help prompted me
to quit feeling so sorry for myself and realize how
lucky I was. Within our community was a clinic
called Teens and Family, which would give Mary a
free assessment of problems. She also came up with
the names of two private counselors, either of whom
might be the impartial adult I was seeking to get
Mary to spill out her hidden feelings.

Yes, I was lucky! Think of the neighborhoods
where you can't call a sympathetic police mom and
get her to alert the night police patrol cars to look for
a thirteen-year-old named Mary and bring her home.

My mind began expanding: what if these teenagers
were in one of the bleak inner-city neighborhoods?
My thoughts began to get more global. If teenagers
just have to break rules and test adults, how does it
play with Bosnian teenagers, with thirteen-year-olds
in Saudi Arabia, in South Africa, in cities where they
sleep with guns? Or in Alaska in those frozen parts
where stealing the dog sled and heading toward more
snow is about the only choice a kid has?

I could feel my blood pressure subside. And I
philosophized that about the only real dangers out
here in West Lake Hills were a deer or a crazed
raccoon, separated from her babies, who might attack. By the next morning, I had evolved a plan for
education-in-the-home. I would get a world globe

and at dinner that night, we would whirl it and let the kids guess: What would thirteen be like here, and here, and here?

This seemed sensible—and fun—and might even be productive. I announced this Global Teenagers game at breakfast, and even began by asking, "What are the dangers in West Lake Hills—other than ruining your health or running into the animals of the hill country?"

"The worst danger isn't raccoons or deer but man," Liz pointed out. "A DWI driver loose on the roads could hit you."

I felt we were getting somewhere. Mary looked interested all of a sudden over the cereal bowl. But she remained silent.

Next day, I turned to my favorite reference books in my growing library of books on teenagers, which included *TEEN Is a Four Letter Word; Your Ten- to Fourteen-Year-Old; Preparing for Adolescence.* One book said:

> Thirteen-year-olds are likely to withdraw, break rules, appear sullen in the company of elders, talk extensively to their friends, stay in their rooms with doors closed and locked, refuse to answer your questions, be unfriendly to everyone except other thirteen-year-olds.

Well, the author sure got that right.

There were a couple of plus symptoms. They do bathe often and comb their hair a lot. Then, back to the negatives:

> They let their grades drop. And they actually enjoy being the bad guy in school, even trying to get into detention hall.

All of these fit Mary perfectly. Last semester she brought in five A's and one B, and this semester she was flunking two subjects. And she was at this very time in detention hall for four days because she refused to take off her new dark gangsterish glasses when the teacher asked her.

An old memory clicked. I remembered a day when I, at thirteen, led half a dozen friends astray, leaving school to hitchhike to a downtown store. And I thought of something Fannie Hurst wrote about her favorite teacher, an assistant principal who headed detention hall. Mr. Schuyler was so sympathetic when Fanny was sent up for reading the wrong books in class—like the Brontës or Mark Twain— that he would have marvelous visits with her and urge her to expand her mind. She was intrigued and often misbehaved, she wrote, so she would get to see and talk with Mr. Schuyler again.

Mary's assistant principal, a wise but firm man, and I were becoming fast friends through conversations about Mary's misdemeanors. By the end of school we were on a first-name basis.

Normal behavior for thirteen-year-olds or not, I couldn't keep on being awakened by the police who had found her somewhere. I was worried, really worried, and I had to do something besides try to separate her from her friends, which seemed impossible since they were all in the same class at school.

Three patterns of her behavior worried me particularly: smoking cigarettes surreptitiously, sneaking out of the house, and never—or rarely ever—acknowledging my instructions or even my existence.

I tried to enlist Tommy's help. He had been her big brother and protector all her life, until he became fifteen and started driving. But he still was my best source on Mary and how to handle her current rebellion.

"It's just a phase," Tommy repeated. "I have noticed even when Mary is acting sorta weird, she uses her head."

I didn't think I could wait the phase out.

"I was like that," said Tommy's friend, Parker, as he eavesdropped from the nearby kitchen where he was slathering cream cheese on a bagel.

"Come in and sit down, Parker, maybe you can

throw some light on this," I said. "How did your parents handle it?"

"My father raised me holistically," he said.

That was a first for me. I tried to conjure up what a parent would be like who raised kids "holistically," and suddenly it dawned on me: Today's thirteen-year-olds are the children of the hippie generation, now more flatteringly called baby boomers.

"Did your parents ever live in an ashram or sell clay pipes?" I asked.

"Both," he said. "Now they are very New Age."

"Well, I am Old Age," I retorted. But I was still curious. "What is holistic raising?" I asked him.

"It's sitting down and letting Mary really analyze what motivates her to a certain behavior," Parker replied. "My father would spend long hours doing this with me."

Holistic raising, indeed! By now I noticed that Parker also had a ponytail, and I remembered that his parents managed a hotel out in the Big Bend National Park, at Terlingua, Texas, home of the famous Texas chili cook-off. Mentally I envisioned them with sandals, headbands, and a large dog on a rope. I learned later they are very respected businesspeople who often vote Republican.

I wondered if I was going to have to go back and study the characteristics of the hippie era and thrust Mary, who barely speaks to any of us, into an analysis session? I had two more speeches to write and deliver before the end of the month, and I just didn't have the time. In desperation, I flipped ahead in *Your Ten- to Fourteen-Year-Old* to the chapter on fourteen-year-olds.

> The age of fourteen tends to be a time of verve, vigor, and excitement. Boundless energy combines with optimistic enthusiasm and goodwill to encourage boy or girl to attempt almost anything. Fourteens enjoy friends, enjoy school, and are even interested in community affairs.

I glanced at the calendar. Mary would be fourteen in seven months, ten days, and two hours. I looked ahead to what I was sure would be the longest seven months of my life.

13
((෴))

Raging Hormones

*L*iz has a boyfriend. Mary has started wearing not only lipstick but rouge. Tommy is besieged with phone calls from girls and he talks in a soft voice as though he is a spy. We are entering the sexual danger zone.

To be the first to tell your children about sex, start prenatally, that's my advice. By the time I got around to talking to them about it, they could have taught courses in it.

With all of the new school instructions because of AIDS, as well as rising teenage pregnancy, and sex on TV around the clock, there is no way to escape the sordid side of sex unless you live in a monastery, and even that is not safe anymore. But that's the pope's worry!

What propelled me to face the subject was Diane

Sawyer, who scared me to death with her TV show on teenage sex. In the United States, 75 percent of teenage girls are sexually active (that's the buzzword for screwing around) before they are out of high school. In Japan, it's 5 percent. Well, at least, we are beating the Japanese at something. The Swedes, after a history of sex and saunas in freezing weather, have everything under control—birth control.

What was startling to find in watching Diane Sawyer's interview with American thirteen-year-olds was their willingness to confess on network television that they had "done it," although they did have the grace to look semiembarrassed. Being a teenage sex celebrity on national TV—even for all the wrong reasons—must have been too tempting in this celebrity-nutty world. But I wonder how those girls are going to think about going public in twenty-five years. Suppose they run for Congress? Sam Donaldson is bound to dig up an old tape of the show and put it on TV, and the *National Enquirer* will spread it on page one. No telling what Bill Safire will do.

To the credit of Diane, she asked each of the girls whether they had any regrets. Yes. Each of them wished she had not succumbed to the moment and tried to please a boyfriend. I called Diane, a friend from White House days, to congratulate her on the show. She had a tremendous response to it, she said. Women called in and reported they had talked to their daughters for the first time because of the show.

As far as Liz, Tommy, and Mary were concerned, all I could do was look for an opening and get in my commercials for sexual abstinence. So thanks to Diane I brought it up.

"Abstinence makes the heart grow fonder until you have found the right person in front of the altar," I tell the kids. They groan and tell me that's a lousy pun.

Tommy says adults worry about teenage sex too much. Once when he was about twelve, someone called, and his older sister answered the phone. "There's a girl on the phone, Tommy," she cried. His dad, who had a great sense of humor, yelled out, "Don't forget to wear a condom when you talk."

Talk about overanxiety!

Out in this neighborhood, Toody Byrd (yep, that's her name) is our wisest counselor on what to do to slow down the raging hormones, since she has weathered thirty years as a high-school teacher and consultant. Toody tells me not to wait until sex comes up. Pitch right in and let them know the code of the house, she says, giving them a few lines to use with their peers, like "I choose to wait until I have a serious relationship." And then hope to God they will use them.

Most septuagenarians like me were virgins at the

altar. Or they had to go around wearing a big red A on their foreheads. In the 1920s, sex was called making love. Today it's just called sex, which takes away a lot—love, for instance. And that's what it should be about.

"If God had wanted you to enjoy your loins only, he would have given you a tail and reduced the size of your brain," I tell them. "But he wanted you to know love—real love—and not limit you to lust. That's the difference." My regret, I explain, is that romance is virtually forgotten.

What I need to do is try to persuade these teenagers not to trade future happiness for two minutes of pleasure. I discussed it with a number of realistic mothers who gave me some recommendations:

· Show them a film of a child being born.
· Make them think about what they really gain by giving in. What do they have to lose?
· Give them a home test. If they answer no to the following questions, they're in charge of their lives.
  Is someone lobbying me?
  Is this really who I want to be?
  Am I willing to risk the death warrant of AIDS?
  Can I take on the responsibility of a small, demanding human being?

I found these hints to be helpful. And the kids seem to listen. My ever-ready cynical friends didn't disappoint, either. "Teach them to masturbate," one advised.

I thought the best possible instruction would come from literature on the subject. My sister-in-law Jean gave me the same material the school gives future home science teachers. Included was an eight-sided (that's right, eight-sided) view of a male penis. Liz turned red, Tommy laughed, and Mary didn't look up from MTV.

Sex did, however, serve as an ice-breaker, and the kids and I started talking more about life and watching more life on TV together. Our favorite show is *Northern Exposure.* During a passionate scene with Maggie and Joel, I commented that they shouldn't be having sex because they're not married.

Mary replied, "So what?"

That's a common response with kids today. Anything goes! TV is disgraceful on the subject. One program featured fashionable sex: combat boots with evening wear. Wild music in the background.

They didn't even blush when they watched it.

I know I can't hope to convince them that my "nice versus naughty" view of morals is the right view. Too much has happened in the world to make the ethics of sixty years ago valid in their lives. But neither can I surrender those ethics myself and embrace today's carnal view of sex, however much I want them to see me as relevant.

After all, I remember what love is. And perhaps the best I can do for these healthy young animals shedding the skin of their childhood is to keep sharing that memory with them in the hope that the idea will take root that there is something out there waiting for them better than anything they could know at their young ages.

14

I Had a Dream

A year into each other's lives, we were all growing. Mary was learning what it is to be a teenager; Liz and Tommy were learning what it is to be adults.

I'm still learning what it is to be a mother in the nineties. I worry not only about the kids, but about every creature on God's earth. My advice to anyone is do not have a digital clock at your bedside, because you know *exactly* what time everything happens. One night the kids were all in bed by eleven thirty-eight P.M., but my sex-crazed raccoons were still out prowling around. Three-nineteen A.M. and still no raccoons. Should I go out and look for them? I spent the entire night worrying until they finally came plodding in at five forty-two A.M.

With the kids' increasing independence came new

interests and real regularity about getting to school on time, about homework, and about the family routine in general.

With the awarding of driver's licenses to the older two, suddenly spring break meant more than hanging around the malls and watching television.

Tommy had an invitation to go to Mexico with friends he had had since grammar school. So we packed him up for a spring break getaway. Saying good-bye, I felt like my mother had when my brother Tom set out to hitchhike through Mexico at eighteen. She had done her best to talk him out of it, but he was a Mexico enthusiast, was fluent in the language, and had friends in Mexico City. My mother was frantic when she didn't hear from him for two weeks. When he finally called in, it was after he had begun to recover from a severe bout of Montezuma's Revenge, which he said had been Pancho Villa's Revenge also.

Remembering this story, I decided to add some Lomotil to Tommy's suitcase and gave him my international phonecard number for telephoning often. I was also glad he didn't want to hitchhike and was going in a reliable car and with plenty of money.

Liz, however, decided for her spring break she would go someplace with spice—New Orleans. I thought she, too, would go in a friend's reliable car. Not so, I learned after the fact. A group from her school, Kirby Hall, started on their eight-hour trek to Louisiana, and just outside Austin the "reliable" car started chugging. The kids, more computer literate than car literate, did know enough to recognize a sick car when they heard it. So they came home. Not wanting to be deterred, they decided to take Liz's worn-out pickup.

I asked her afterward if she was scared or ever thought it wouldn't make it.

"No," she replied. "It was like being in a great *film noire*. A real rite of passage."

That's Liz. She puts *everything* in the context of a movie. A trip to my kind and gentle dentist reminded her of the scene from *Little Shop of Horrors* with a demented Steve Martin using a jackhammer on Bill Murray's teeth. I found that I could use movies or television shows to communicate with her. It was something to which we both could relate.

In fact, one night we were watching *Mystic Pizza*, a movie about teenagers working in a pizza parlor. It struck me that Liz was old enough, she was smart enough, and, doggone it, she needed a job. A pizza place would be perfect—and there was even one close to Kirby Hall. She must have been inspired by the movie, because she went there the very next day and got a job.

The job really helped Liz. She met more people— even acquired a new boyfriend—and found the liberty of having her own spending money. Seeing her undergo such a change prompted Tommy to get a job also.

So the routine was set. Liz often worked after school, usually getting home about six in the evening (I worried about her homework, but she seemed to be keeping up with her classes.) Tommy picked up Mary from her school and they would get home about four.

One day, though, everyone got confused. Liz and Mary decided that they would go shopping after school. Since he didn't have to pick Mary up at school, Tommy would go to the library to finish a paper. I had rehearsal with the Bay at the Mooners for our appearance at a chic little rest home we called "Curtains." Actually that wasn't its name, but when we looked it over, that's what it appeared to be, and we decided we would have to sing LOUD.

When I got home, the answering machine was flashing. It was Mary. No one had picked her up—something that had happened once or twice before with Tommy—and she was at Amy's Ice Cream calmly eating her way through a banana split. I went to pick her up but was amazed that Liz had forgotten her.

Mary and I waited at home for Liz, but she didn't come. It was five, then six, and seven, but no Liz. It was getting dark, and I started calling around to her friends and the pizza shop. No luck. I reached her school's headmistress, who was home by now, and she called the janitor at school to search the building. In a minute he called me back. Liz had just come downstairs from the lounge, where she had been sound asleep all afternoon.

"Sleep isn't that important," I admonished her when she got home. "I read that if you added all the eight-hour nights together for the normal lifetime, it would mean we sleep twenty-five years of our life. Do you want to spend twenty-five years like Rip Van Winkle?"

"It wouldn't be so bad," she added, and sure enough, she turned in right after dinner that night.

By the time I got to bed it was midnight and after the third toss and turn, I took a sleeping pill and fell into a deep slumber and a dream-filled night.

I began to hear sounds and to see a fuzzy vision of myself in a flowing gown—size six—wandering about the house. I heard Mary in the kitchen. She seemed to be preparing a scrumptious dinner. She had learned to cook and she was preparing a fabulous pot-au-feu.

As I walked past her, she said, "I have mastered the art of French cooking, Aunt Liz. From now on, every night will be a gourmet feast. Your cooking days are over." I walked on down to the living room and there was Liz arranging all my books by the Dewey decimal system.

"I have sworn off Stephen King until I organize these books so we can find everything," she said. "Do you want the transcendentalists next to the existentialists?"

From the garden came the clack of the pruning shears and clippers. Tommy had also developed a "domestic art"—gardening! I looked out and rubbed my eyes. He had turned Grass Roots into a veritable Hampton Court. Not just bluebonnets and gay feathers but . . . topiary! trimmed into a magical menagerie of green animals.

I was startled to see a delegation of teens at the door. The spokesperson was Jessica, she of the Great Auto Caper Incident, "Liz, we know how tight things are, so we have a suggestion. Why don't you let all of us leechy teenage hanger-ons do all of your cleaning, laundry, grocery shopping, and maintenance from now on. You've done so much for us, we just want a way of paying you back and showing our gratitude. Plus you can save money because we wouldn't think of charging you a cent."

The alarm clock was ringing and seemed to have been ringing for a looong time. I sat upright. It was seven-fifty A.M. and the kids were going to be late for school. I hurried to call them but to my amazement they *were* up, dressed, and in the kitchen getting breakfast.

Can it be that the times they are a-changing?

I have to be honest. I have been hearing more thank-you's. They have been calling home to let me know where they are. And I was really touched when they actually were concerned about me recently when I had to stay over in Dallas after a bumpy landing. I can't stand turbulence and I dread flying even though I have to do it. As I once said, and the *Reader's Digest* gave me twenty-five dollars for the quote, "The Wright Brothers were wrong." I stand on that even though I admit that you can't operate today without flying. I have friends staked out in Dallas who know they may get a sudden call: May I spend the night with you? So it was last week. It was several hours before I could get in from Dallas airport to bed down at the Tillers.

Finally I did call. And they sounded relieved. "Why didn't you call earlier?" Mary said, picking up on my line. I quickly apologized and promised never to fail again.

I am beginning to come around to believe that some of the teen traits that bother me are not unique to Tommy, Mary, and Liz, but simply go with the teenage territory.

"Every teenager in the world drops clothes, looks sullen, remains untalkative, but there are virtues," a parent said. "They really do care about the world. This is the eco-culture. Just wait." Political addict that I am, I wondered if a giant convention—say—

something like the United Nations of Teenagers—would be able to pass resolutions against the bad habits. But I dismissed that idea when I visualized a giant hall of teens taking over the world. We would be at their mercy. This eco-culture, which carries picket signs to save the rainforests and battles for clean air and water, might make those good things happen—but with them would come a world of clothes strewn around from New York City to Delhi, cold drink cans clogging the clean streams, and boom boxes clearing the forests of birds and animals.

Animals would be fleeing the planet just like they fled the forest fire in the movie about Bambi.

Not yet. They are not ready to take over the world yet.

15

Pomp and Consequence

*A*lmost every parent has done it. And here I was doing it ... *again* ... writing school assignments for a child who puts off everything until the last minute. The way I figure it, I should have already gotten three high-school diplomas, not to mention the Golden R Reading Award.

The problem was Liz, who failed to come up with most of her assignments in the Literary Genres class. She didn't tell me and she didn't worry. She just kept reading her Stephen King novels, which don't count for anything except a lot of mayhem. A stern call from her teacher informed me that she wasn't going to graduate if she didn't produce the following:

- a four-page paper on George Orwell
- a four-page study of Faulkner's characterization in *The Sound and the Fury*
- a three-page analysis of Ray Bradbury's future in *The Pedestrian*
- a six-page paper on women in the military
- a three-page comparison of Freud's theories and Margaret Mead's feminism
- a seven-page research paper on King Arthur.

To emphasize the panic, this was Thursday; her graduation ceremony was Sunday. Even with my lousy math, I count that as four days.

Something had to be done fast if she was going to enter summer school in New York. I had already paid the entrance fee by telephone with my Visa card. I couldn't watch the money go down the drain and I couldn't bear for Liz to miss out on graduating with her classmates. She was plenty smart, but completely unapplied, undisciplined—well, infuriatingly unreliable about homework. What percentage of teenagers are lost in the cloud of their own dreams? I knew that Liz was dreaming of New York, of studying to be a cinematographer. But I also knew she was blind to deadlines. So I had to rally!

All my old instincts as a crash ghostwriter for presidents, first ladies, and occasional cabinet members surfaced, and I quickly summoned a team to avoid having to read or reread the books. Paula and her boyfriend, Riley, would take on the longest paper, about King Arthur. We would all work on the papers covering Freud/Mead and women in the military. I would pursue the analysis of William Faulkner's characters. And we would tackle George Orwell together. Ten-nine-eight-seven . . . ! This was like a countdown at Cape Canaveral. Everything depended on getting the work done and into the hands of her teacher. The situation was serious, so serious that Nancy, Liz's mother, who generally takes things in her stride, came and joined in to make hourly runs to the library and the office supply store.

My home office became a frantic scene of two computers—mine and Paula's—both working with Liz, who sat sipping a diet Coke in the lounge chair, Stephen King still in hand. We would interrupt her occasionally and prod her to provide any thoughts she might have for the belated homework. It was maddening. If we were patient enough, she would come up with statements and ideas gleaned from her classes. But our patience soon ran out. I grabbed the fat paperback out of her hand and pointed her to one of the teams scurrying around on her behalf. She was going to do at least some of the work here, damn it!

We had to move fast to get it all done. I was on the phone tapping instant knowledge wherever I could. No literature professor at the University of Texas was safe. Nor were friends and neighbors who kept their home libraries better organized than I did.

"Which Faulkner character is the easiest to describe? What was he trying to say?" I fired questions at a full professor with life tenure at the University of Texas. In five minutes, she had given me the answer so I could write the damn four pages. No one was spared—my neighbor Henrietta stopped her city meeting on zoning down at city hall to rush home and bring me an old summary on Faulkner from her long-ago college days. She's the kind of person who saves everything and knows exactly where it is. Thank God!

I even tapped my old friends from the women's movement—Betty Friedan in Sag Harbor and Pat Schroeder in Washington, D.C. What insight could they give me on the historical role of women in the military? Hooray! They knew plenty! Women were there in the American Revolution, shaving their heads to disguise themselves as men so they could join brothers or lovers.

"Of course," Betty added, "after they were wounded, the disguise was all over and they either went home or to the cemetery depending upon their condition. Actually, one is buried at West Point, though you'd never know it if you left it to the West Point guides."

By Friday night we were exhausted, but the words

were falling into shape in my personal computer-land. (And Liz was almost through her Stephen King novel.) I learned some things, too. Mostly that Faulkner is really difficult to read. It is hard to keep your characters straight when you are meeting them through the eyes of a halfwit (the brother, not Faulkner).

Late Saturday, we were done, papers polished and ready to hand to Mr. Literature Professor, the demanding teacher who expected his students to do what they are told. Can you imagine? I knew he was right, but why hadn't he warned me earlier there was a problem? By now I was angry at him as well as Liz.

Early Sunday, I don't think it was much past seven in the morning, Nancy came by to help get the papers to the professor. It was now only hours before the graduation ceremony. We had the address of an apartment about ten miles across town where the professor lived. I drove Nancy in my car because I didn't trust her van, which is often out of gas and breaks down frequently. In fact, I was in such a state of panic, I even considered hiring a garage mechanic to go along just in case anything happened to my car. We set out feeling tense. I sensed the importance of the mission, feeling a little like my ancestor Dr. John Sutherland, when he rode out of the Alamo to Gonzales, Texas, to try to rally volunteers and save the day for Texas. He barely made it in time to get thirty-two volunteers, but the Alamo fell anyway. I didn't want the same fate for Liz. These thoughts were racing through my head as we dashed across town and then started searching for the right apartment in a maze of look-alike apartments.

Excelsior! This looked like the spot, and Nancy took the papers and headed for the the final destination, Number 203. In about fifteen *looong* minutes, she reappeared smiling. She had awakened a very sleepy and truly disgusted teacher who now had to grade the papers before the graduation services started at two P.M.

We raced home to wake up the three kids, who prefer sleeping in on Sundays to anything else: not even *Beavis and Butt-head* can get them up early. They don't blink an eye about sleeping through Sunday school. Please God, forgive me, for I know what I am doing. I do not have the strength to make them get up on Saturday and Sunday when they get up every other day at seven A.M. The battle is too hard. And it is my day to stay in bed with Charles Kuralt (electronically, of course, courtesy of CBS).

How come I always went to Sunday school, even won a medal for perfect attendance, and I can't get these kids there? All the psychology books tell me we're leaving a huge gap in this generation's spiritual development. At the very least children should get a good solid dose of religion so they have something to rebel against later—and the moral fiber to return to it. We are—some spa expert told me—a piece of pie, divided into three parts: physical, emotional, and spiritual. When she said that, I tried to think of myself as a piece of pie—coconut cream—and promptly got hungry.

Graduation time came at a lovely Lutheran church. I spent the first fifteen minutes on my knees, trying to thank God for getting us through this ordeal. We were all in our pews. Liz, well rested and dressed in a beautiful daffodil-yellow evening gown, was outside somewhere with the other graduates. She had, of course, failed to buy the right shoes, but a friend was bringing a pair for her to put on at the church. If they didn't fit or if the friend met a terrible fate on the way—a car crash, a plane falling on her, even a clock with the wrong time (I've got to stop worrying and working myself into a frenzy of fantasies)—Liz would appear in the beautiful daffodil-yellow gown with God knows what on her feet.

The organist began "Pomp and Circumstance." I graduated from high school to that melody myself; it's a regal tune that triggers tears. It did then, and it did now. The processional began, led by the headmistress. I looked back down the aisle, and there at the rear I spotted Mr. Literature Professor and winked at him. His piercing eyes gave no clue, but I could tell he was already lost in thought of heading for the beach or the mountains as soon as the ceremony was over and he could flee from these irresponsible kids.

The graduates passed our pew, and there was Liz, really the most beautiful one. I didn't dare look at her shoes for fear it would spoil my moment of pleasure in case she had borrowed Mary's green combat boots. Her name was called. We cheered from our pew—Mary, Tommy, Nancy, my brother and sister-in-law George and Jean, Paula and Riley.

The speaker—it was the head of the Salvation Army, which I hope is not prophetic—began: "These students stand here with the support and help of their family and friends."

Paula and I rolled our eyes knowingly.

Commencement speakers try so hard to make their words different, but how many ways are there to say Do your best, We believe in you, and The world needs you? I once read Russell Baker's advice to a graduating class: "The world is out there waiting for you," he said. "Don't go."

Again, my mind went back to my own high-school graduation in 1938. A rabbi was the speaker, a beloved, funny man who sprinkled jokes along the way, but who was dead serious when he beaded in on us with his real message: "Just remember, my young friends, the so-called New Morality is just a new name for the same old Immorality."

I remember my reaction at the time: I clamped my legs tight together and never unclenched them throughout life. Well, maybe now and then—legally speaking.

After the ceremony, Mr. Literature Professor handed Liz her papers showing she had eked through and passed. She barely glanced at them as she hurried on to the graduates' reception. Paula and I pounced on the papers to find out how we had done on our team effort. Paula broke into a big smile. Her treatise on King Arthur did best—an A. There was also an A for "Feminism and the Military," but for the rest of the papers, C's. Former presidential speechwriter and best-selling author now a humiliated C-level high-school student! A favorite saying came readily to mind—"No good deed goes unpunished." That night while Liz was partying with her class, I borrowed one of her Stephen King books to find out what was going on in the literary world that I was unaware of. Well, I must confess, Stephen King does hold you.

Since then, my mix of emotions about this adventure has shifted. At the time, the dominant feeling was relief that we got Liz through it and down the aisle to her diploma. There was a dash of excitement over marshaling the writing effort to victory. And with it all, a kernel of guilt. Only a kernel. After all, I hadn't been responsible for her when she was supposed to learn the habits of time management.

Some of my childless friends were indignant, however, "You should have let her fail," they said. "However worthy your motives, this was a rip-off of the educational system."

More than anything else, I am troubled by the effect this might have had on Liz herself. We got her diploma for her, but at what cost to her self-reliance and ultimately her self-respect? I am disturbed when I consider how she will handle the next crisis in her life. Will she believe that she can ignore her responsibilities, secure in the assumption that someone else will take them on?

One week after graduation, Liz stepped on a plane and headed for New York City to live with her half-sister, Deirdre. Liz's eyes were dancing with excitement when we said good-bye, her memo book full of instructions and phone numbers.

As my namesake said her final good-bye, she turned and put her arms around me and said, "I love you, Liz."

It was the first time she had ever said that to me. Now, when we talk long distance—once or twice a week—"I love you" is her sign-off. The words are worth waiting for.

16
(⦿)

Don't Puff
the Magic Dragon

 iz's departure left the house less crowded, but it felt emptier, too. I noticed that Mary was more and more alone as Tommy went out in the car with his friends. After school and on weekends, Mary was restless and bored. She wanted to spend more time with friends. I was lucky if she even told me their names. Generally when she talked about "hanging out with friends," they remained nameless.

More and more, I read frightening headlines and heard newscasts about suicide, guns, and drugs in our town. I began to realize that this is Heartache Time in America. The sixties were tame compared to the nineties. At least in the sixties, there was a cause, Vietnam, and the protest marches for peace. And in the sixties when someone got angry, he didn't pull out a gun and shoot you.

Today unbridled sex, drugs, and guns are accepted as part of the scene, and the scene is getting younger and closer. Little wonder—take a look at today's role models. Children don't look up to astronauts, presidents, authors, or opera stars. Celebrity worship is rampant and ridiculous. A magazine cover features Roseanne Arnold dressed only in a black lace corset, her legs grossly spread across a chair. We see a TV show of Michael Jackson grabbing his crotch to frenzied music and then learn he's accused of molesting a child. Madonna makes hand motions that make Mae West look like a nun. And on an average Saturday morning, cartoon characters punch, karate-kick, and kill their way through our breakfast hour.

We talk of human values but the walls keep tumbling down around us. Am I, now surrogate to three teenagers, simply to accept the current ugly climate? Not over my declining body.

My personal experience with the demons of the nineties began weeks before when Mary came home from school with an announcement.

"I have a theme that's due in four weeks," she said matter-of-factly.

"What's it on?" I pursued.

"Well, the teacher put about thirty subjects on the

blackboard including crime, violence, recycling. I picked suicide."

"Suicide!" I tried not to shout, adding, "It sounds like a grim subject to me."

I was indignant at a teacher who would list such negative theme subjects when many positive ones are possible.

Suicide scared me, especially because one of Mary's friends had recently been admitted to the local mental hospital for taking four or five pills from her mother's tranquilizer bottle.

Wracking my brain for a casual reply to Mary, I quoted the Dorothy Parker poem on the subject.

> Guns are unlawful;
> Nooses give;
> Gas smells awful;
> You might as well live.

That was as light as I could get about suicide. If she was going to use this as her theme, I was going to help with her research.

We found alarming statistics in my growing library on teenagers, and I asked her to read them aloud.

" 'Eighteen adolescents commit suicide in the U.S. each day,' " she read. " 'Suicide is the number-two killer of adolescents.' " With her typical logic Mary stopped to ask, "What's the number-one killer?"

"Television mania," I offered.

A few days later Mary returned from school. "I'm not doing suicide for my project any longer," she said.

"How come?" I inquired.

"The project is about the future and Mr. White says suicide has no future."

"What is your subject then?" I asked.

"Drugs," she said matter-of-factly.

"I'm sorry that drugs have a future," I replied.

But it set me thinking. Too slowly I was learning that to deal with these teenagers I needed an intensive brush-up course on the MTV generation. I was fifty during Woodstock. Timothy Leary never tempted me. Smoking grapevine and skinny dipping on April Fool's Day with the girls was as madcap as I got. As for heavy depression, I learned at Sunday school that the best way to stop thinking about yourself is to do something for someone else.

All in all, I am so out of the drug culture that if someone said, "I'm gonna take a trip," I would get him a suitcase.

Mary's assignment to do a paper on drugs prompted many discussions on what is happening in our own neighborhood. I became worried about the casual attitude of both Tommy and Mary.

"Everyone does it."

"Drugs are everywhere, even in our schools."

"Marijuana is not habit forming. It is a paternalistic law that makes it illegal."

In an historical note, Tommy added, "The first Native Americans smoked peyote."

"They also danced around naked," I replied.

From the beginning—when these children came here—I had made it plain that any drugs or alcohol were unacceptable. This was a good time to reinforce the prerequisites. So heading it off at the pass as well as helping Mary research her paper became a mission with me. Apparently there are no safe neighborhoods. Not even monasteries and prisons. If you are alive, you are involved.

I checked out the experiences of friends who are parents of teenagers. Most of the parents of Tommy's and Mary's friends are in their forties, can tolerate grunge music, and have personally done drugs sometime during their own growing up. That has two advantages: They know the harm and they know the clues for detecting it. Some are seriously concerned, enough to run regular room searches when their teenager isn't home.

"To hell with privacy," one dad said; "there are no privacy rules when you are a footsoldier in the war on drugs."

"Pockets! Search the pockets of pants and shirts,"

another said. "Between mattresses is also a favorite place, and if you are looking for hidden booze, don't forget the toilet tank."

"The dealers are getting trickier," someone else said. "If you spot a page of stamps with little animals on them, don't lick them. They're acid! But they are made to look as innocent as a Disneyland game."

It occurred to me somebody could make a fortune renting out search-and-sniff dogs to parents.

Because I wanted them to realize just how serious even a one-time offense could be, I invited a friend who is a criminal juvenile lawyer to come answer any questions they might have. We were going to talk over the dinner table. He brought along a judge who faces kids with drug problems every day and hands out the sentences.

On Friday evening the two men showed up. I couldn't believe my eyes when the judge came in with an earring in one ear and a long ponytail down his back. I secretly wondered if he had come in disguise to better relate to teenagers. I was transfixed hearing the truths about drugs as they talked, and even the restless teenagers were listening.

Mary told about a friend who had been suspended from school for three days and sent to juvenile court because a bag of marijuana had been found on him. She felt that it was unfair because the suspension came at exam time.

"What did they do to him in court?" the judge asked.

"They gave him twenty hours of community service," Mary replied.

"He was lucky, Mary. Do you realize what would have happened if he had been caught with marijuana twenty miles north of here in Williamson County?" he asked.

No reply.

"Well, he would be in juvenile detention, still waiting for a court date."

"You know," the lawyer spoke up, "just today I had a client who is a first-year law student who got busted when he was eighteen."

Mary and Tommy were tuned in.

"This guy came before the state bar for a routine certification and the bar booted his application," he continued.

"Why?" queried Tommy.

"Because he had a criminal record for marijuana possession. A person with a record can't be bonded."

"But he was only eighteen," Mary said. "How old is he now?"

"Twenty-three, with a wife and a new baby, but that doesn't matter," he replied. "If you get caught as an adult, your record stays with you your whole life. When they're throwing dust onto your grave at the age of ninety-six, you'll still have a criminal record."

I decided to share one particularly horrifying tale that I had heard. A young man had been getting stoned since his early teenage years, always maintaining it was his choice to do what he wanted to do. When he was eighteen he had an accident while driving high and ended up killing a young girl.

"Mary," the lawyer asked, "how would you like to be eighteen and have to live the rest of your life knowing you killed someone?"

"I wouldn't do that," Mary contended.

"But," I spoke up, "you don't have that option if you're not in control of your mental and physical self."

"Come on, Liz," Tommy admonished, "those kinds of stories don't happen in real life. It's movie material."

"You are so wrong, Tommy," Paula said in a husky, low tone.

Something in her voice must have hit a chord in Tommy because he actually turned to listen to Paula as she continued.

"About ten years ago, my cousin Michael was driving home in his pickup on a two-lane highway." She sat quietly twisting her hands with anguish as she told the story. "As he approached a curve in the road, he noticed this small car coming toward him at a really high speed. The driver, we learned later, had

been experimenting with a combination of marijuana and some over-the-counter drugs.

"Michael had just enough time to react and
jerked the pickup toward the ditch, but he couldn't
avoid the impact. The car broadsided the pickup
with so much force the pickup 'horseshoed' around
the car. The driver was killed instantly, lucky fool.
Michael wasn't so lucky. They care-flighted his unconscious body to Dallas. For five months my family stood by helpless. We held his hand, cried at the
hopelessness, and prayed desperately for him to
come out of the coma. He died Christmas Eve of
that year.

"I find it so hard to believe that anyone could be so
stupid to risk their life and others' by doing drugs,
Tommy," she said with conviction. "Things like this
do happen. It could happen to you."

The judge looked across at Mary. "So, what are you
going to do if someone offers you a joint?" he asked
her.

"I'm going to say no," she said.

"Why?"

"Because it's illegal and can cause damage," she
replied.

"Mary, that's a very mature decision."

I could see Mary was pleased with the acknowledgment of her maturity. She sat a little higher in her

chair, concentrated a little harder on the conversation.

"And what about you, Tommy?" the judge asked.

Tommy said, "I'm looking at music for my solace."

"That's wise," the judge commended. "I've always felt that if you have great potential—which, Tommy, you and Mary both have—then you have the most to lose if you do drugs."

Tommy and Mary appreciated the compliment and, I think, understood what he meant. I hope this is the only round we have with the drug demon. I've heard so much about chemical composition of drugs and sad tales about the offenders that, frankly, I've OD'd on the drug scene. I've learned that all a parent can do is present the facts about drugs and the dire consequences of using them. The final decision lies in each person's own hands.

17

School Daze

*N*ow that we have our own round table on social issues, virtually a little Aspen Institute in Texas, each meal is a social discussion. We choose topics as a theme for dinner, like "What is the most pressing problem facing the world today?"

Mary loves to stump me with scientific questions. One evening at dinner she said, "Liz, how many stars does our solar system have?"

I thought a long time, trying to give it the best shot I could, but I've always been a lousy science student. "I don't know, Mary, a few trillion?"

"Wrong," she said. "Just one, and we revolve around it."

She has considered being an astronomer and she'd make a good one with her quick mind that understands black holes and Einstein's theories.

Mary has a dancer's body—lithe and graceful—and she recently started taking jazz dance classes twice a week, which I hope will widen her circle of friends.

For the first time, Tommy asked me to come attend his school on parents' night—where the parents become students and move from class to class, each lasting five minutes with two minutes to move in and out. The other parents, most in their early forties and used to morning jogging and working out, had no trouble. I was the cow's tail.

Most of the teachers I met were really trying. Tommy says sometimes they try him needlessly. But I found them young, full of enthusiasm, and even willing to write their home phone numbers on the blackboard in case you wanted to call them day or night. I also was impressed with the heavy participation by parents. All the seats were filled, and finding such strong parental interest is bound to make a difference to the teachers.

Tommy took Latin and learned how to sing "Happy Birthday" in Latin for starters. The teacher told us that later in the year they would have a Roman dinner for the class and their parents—togas optional.

But it was language arts that captured his attention, and he was eager for me to meet Mrs. Flatau, who teaches it and is also attractive and brainy. She is good at getting grants and applied for one so her classes could get computers. She won it. Ultimately the students will be able to tap various university professors and experts in many parts of the country. They also have access to Prodigy and other reference sources.

Today's high-school students are tackling the great books, which we didn't have available to us until college. And there is a big emphasis on poetry, which helps to soften the world.

Teachers make such a difference. It only takes one or two to turn you on to learning. That has happened to Tommy and I see signs of it happening to Mary.

There are amazing stories of people who overcame personal obstacles to make it to the top. I told the kids about three friends, all nationally known now, who had lots going against them but conquered it all. Ray Marshall, whom I knew when he was a secretary of labor to President Carter, told me that he was raised in a Baptist orphanage in Mississippi and taught in an orphanage school where three volunteer teachers taught eight classes.

"It was a retired judge who opened my eyes to learning and to the evils of racism," he said, "and who believed in me."

Another orphanage-educated friend, humor columnist Art Buchwald, told me he learned to make people laugh because as a kid he was the shortest one in the orphanage and needed to keep from being bullied. He did it by comedy.

James Michener never knew his parents, but was raised in a foster home by a Mrs. Michener who read to the children every night, in that way making him a seeker of knowledge. "When the Carnegie Library opened in Doylestown, Pennsylvania, I went down, got a card, and read everything in the library. Later I was told by the librarian that the first two cards issued were to Margaret Mead and me," Michener said.

Tommy and Mary met James Michener when he came for dinner before departing for Florida. He would have been perfect for our next project. We were thinking about creating a Live Poets' Society and inviting some of our poetry-composing friends. The teens were really pressing for it, and I agreed on meeting for reading poetry on a regular basis. Tommy called ten of his friends, Mary invited a few friends, and I asked some of mine to come for a buffet dinner and poetry reading. Everyone would bring something to read, preferably of their own creation.

On opening night, the MTV generation arrived starving and pounced on the food with relish, while we antiques sat discussing one-day denture making. We got all the generational introductions over, visited over food, and then settled down before the fireplace with a good light on a reading stand, still a little fidgety about how the evening would unfold. I appointed myself emcee to call on the various readers, although Tommy felt this was unnecessary. He envisioned the event as Quaker-meeting style, where you sit in silence until the spirit moves you. I suspected we would sit silently all evening if someone didn't take over.

I had taken out the insurance of asking my cowboy poet friend, H. C. Carter, to be on hand to read his poetry first and give the kids courage. Sporting his jeans, polished boots, and Stetson, plus the biggest belt buckle in the state, H.C. cuts a picturesque figure and knows it. H.C. was fabulous. He was well fortified with his poems, and the kids immediately took to him. H.C. read, with gusto, one of his own poems about the West. The poem occasionally scanned, and sometimes rhymed.

But my fears that these sixteen- and seventeen-year-olds would be shy about reading their poetry aloud in front of older adults were needless. Hands went up around the room to be the next, and what unfolded was some rather good stuff—in some cases cynical, as teenagers are, and in others wildly visionary about the land, or even the rhythm of the city. Tommy read his own words, which were filled with raw images and poetic language.

Mary read a couple of poems written by her father. As I listened to her reading those words so familiar to me, I was caught off guard and found myself hurting inside. I turned my head so no one could see the tears. I miss my brother, but that day I realized how much of his love for poetry lives in his children.

I had a hard time getting my own turn in. I read, too, not an original poem, but one by Jenny Joseph that I identify with. It says in part: "When I am an old lady I shall wear purple, with a red hat which doesn't go and doesn't suit me."

Hearing the works of the teens was more exciting to all of us. They really were live poets. I had not given them credit for their sensitivity and willingness to talk about feelings.

By the end of the evening, the two generations had blended. One of Tommy's young friends was teaching H.C. about rockabilly—a combination of rock and honkytonk music—and one of my friends was showing Mary and her friends how to jitterbug.

What started off as a Grand Canyon Generation Gap had been bridged with a little poetry, a lot of food, and a pinch of magic.

18

⟪⟨∞⟩⟫

Fourteen—At Last!

*I*t was only two weeks away—Mary's long-awaited fourteenth birthday, when I expected everything to change for the better. I wanted to make the most of it, since, as far as I was concerned, it would usher out the bad habits and bring in some wonderful new ones.

"It's not going to be like someone turning a switch on me and making a miracle," Mary said in her own defense.

But I was sure that all the testing of the limits I had endured, all the obsession with one and only one friend, would end. So I set out to mark the move from thirteen to fourteen in a big way.

I had as much fun planning the party as I had giving it. I really don't know how the idea dawned, but it happened about four-twenty in the morning, according to my digital clock, as I lay thinking how to help Mary find a few more friends. How do you find the right peer group? Typical of thirteen-year-olds is the one-friend fixation. Not only do they have to spend the night on weekends but, once home from school, they are on the phone to one another for hours. I was itchy to make fourteen a real step because no one should have to suffer thirteen one day more.

Roots! I thought. Mary needs to know about her deep roots in Texas. She needs to know there is adventure beyond the malls and movies. At first, I didn't dare tell her we were going to hold her birthday celebration in Salado, the country town where I was born and where my mother—Mary Elizabeth Robertson, for whom Mary is named—was born. The family home, which is only an hour away from our house in Austin, is a gracious antebellum house that looks like something out of *Gone With the Wind* and is still standing after 140 years. It is full of ghost stories and, yes, ghosts. As a child, I heard them when I drifted off to sleep. Ghosts rustled around the twenty-four rooms of that old creaky house, which seemed to settle into the ground when the sun went down. Sometimes I would hear a ghost with boots slowly going up the stairs, one by one, and I knew it must be one of my grandfathers.

Even though we had moved to Austin when I was seven, I spent holidays and summertimes in the family homeplace, enchanted by old tales, loving to be scared as we played in the spooky family cemetery among the old tombstones with their flowery epitaphs. We cousins even made some of the dead ancestors our pretend playmates—particularly two little girls who died of scarlet fever and whose portraits hang in the old parlor on a wall opposite a framed letter from Robert E. Lee to my great-grandfather.

I was eager for Mary to know about her own pioneer family and about her grandmother whose name she bore. Family legends and stories, I think, give you a sense of continuity and belonging. Who was to tell her if I didn't? Maybe a birthday slumber party would be the trick—a slumber party at the picturesque old Stagecoach Inn, with a birthday cake at the Robertson homeplace. The plan grew like an MTV production.

I tapped my Aunt Lucille Robertson, who lives at the homeplace and is the keeper of the family flame; Bryant Reeves, who knows how to make things festive; and Grace Jones, who runs an ultra-high-couture shop in a town that once offered only calico. Unlike the big department stores, Grace Jones's shop offers you a comfortable couch, a Coca-Cola or coffee, and dresses that range from $175 to $9,000. She once sold three $9,000 dresses in one day. In this one-horse town that's a miracle.

They all joined in the planning along with Tyler Fletcher, whose grandmother owns the quaint bookstore. He promised to come tell some Indian tales. Geneva Aiken, manager of the Stagecoach Inn, gave me a good rate, so I lined up a suite for the girls and a room next door for me. The suite had an icebox so Dr Peppers and snacks were in order.

By the time we set out, the schedule was filled and I handed an itinerary to each girl. They must have thought it was strange to get a printed party schedule. But these old advance-woman instincts die hard.

Arrive at 2:00 P.M., check into Stagecoach Inn.

2:30: Stroll through Salado to Serenity, a statue of an Indian mermaid, by the springs behind Grace Jones's store.

2:45: Jiggle toes in springs.

3:00: Stroll through gift shops.

4:15: Off to the Robertson house for storytelling and cake-cutting.

6:00: Dinner back at Stagecoach Inn.

7:30: Horse-and-buggy tour of Salado.

8:30: In the suite—card games, CD music, Ouija board.

Next day: Sleep late.

12 noon: Walk to Grace's store, for fashion tips.

1:00 P.M.: Lunch at Browning's Cottage.

2:00: Back to Grace's store for a fashion show. *You* are the models wearing her latest. Beware! Be careful. These clothes are from Milan, Paris, and New York.

4:30: Leave Salado for home, homework, and school.

Mary was unenthusiastic. She invited only one friend at first and I had to prod her until there were two others. Each was asked to bring a bathing suit, a change of clothes, and a family story to share.

I was busy with phone calls and plans. I wanted to herald the new Era of Fourteen when everything is supposed to get better, and there would be "wider cultural interest," according to one of my reference books. Mary's friends were excited. Mary was dragging her feet.

As a child, I was enchanted by Salado, and I thought even city-raised, moviegoing, mall-walking friends might like to hang out there. The town is a picturesque village, nestled along a fast-flowing creek fed by crystal-clear springs out of the limestone rockbed. Watercress—crisp and peppery— grows on either side of the stream. There is Main Street, which, as in so many small Texas towns of a certain vintage, was made the width it took to turn a wagon and an ox-team around, and is now accommodating buses of tourists who want to spend a Saturday or Sunday browsing the antique stores and the gift shops. Salado is human scale, with fifteen hundred residents who ranch or farm or just live happily and serenely. There is one sheriff, a volunteer fire department, and no city government. If something needs to be done, the Salado Chamber of Commerce passes the hat and gets it done. People are so hungry for towns like Salado that they retire there, and as a result, Salado now has three gourmet restaurants and two golf courses laid out by Robert Trent Jones.

When we drove into Salado, Mary and the three friends whom she finally added for the slumber party were excited and hugging each other even though Main Street was virtually deserted.

"Where is everyone?" Mary asked in dismay. "You said there are fifteen hundred people."

She wanted all fifteen hundred crowding the street just like a city mall. But when I gave each girl five dollars and they walked down the street to a candle shop, things improved. There were actually smiles and more jumping up and down and hugging each other. Even Mary. Candles, incidentally, are big with Mary and friends as they like to play their Ouija boards in near-darkness and talk sun signs in candlelight. They wandered down to the springs and saw the statue of Serenity sitting in the creek and raced to get a better look.

Salado is quiet. Quiet is something kids today rarely know. Silence makes them jittery.

I can't say the weekend was a roaring success to anyone but me. However, it did get them away from the city, and they did absorb some history. They loved acting model-like in the expensive clothes as Grace Jones directed them. And Mary truly was quiet and pensive as her Aunt Lucille told her about ancestors who lived in that house. Lucille went all out. We sipped punch out of the cut-glass punch-bowl, three generations old, and ate Mary's birthday cake off the china plates handpainted with flowers and birds by some of her great-aunts.

There were other benefits to that trip to Salado. Freedom to roam for one. There, I didn't worry about traffic or muggers. The girls could browse the stores of that small town, take a late-night buggy ride, or have coffee in the coffee shop at will. Swim or hit the hot tub. They did all those. Next afternoon when we returned to Austin and I dropped them off, there were hugs all around, and some scattered thank-yous.

As Mary and I drove home alone, she fell silent. When we turned the final corner approaching the house she spoke. "Tell me more about my grandmother," she said. This made it all worthwhile.

I knew at that point what my Christmas present would be to her: a collection of photographs of my mother from her teenage years and throughout her life. Mary looks a lot like her. I can only hope that Mary will pick up on her grandmother's fine mind and loving heart as well.

One night a few weeks later, Mary came home happy and receptive to conversation. You can talk, but the teenager's ability to talk while sitting still is nil. Tommy has to drum a foot or use his fingers to beat out a tune on the table. We might be discussing Walt Whitman, or whether he can take off from his weekend job because some rock group is in town, but he can't converse with all limbs still.

I was in bed reading when Mary came into the bedroom and started using my exercise bike with only one foot going round and round. She assured me while she was in clockwise motion that, yes, her math, vocabulary, and English theme on Who Is a Great Teacher? were done to the required point, so I complimented her and proceeded to get my licks in as she twirled. It was a true teenage picture and I wish I'd had a camera to snap it, but it would have had to have been a movie camera.

"Mary, you really have a good brain," I told her. "I've noticed that when you apply it, you get right to the point. There is no wandering off. You pursue the thought in a direct line. That's a gift. Tommy's mind operates with lots of tangents and philosophical thoughts. I bet if you had an aptitude test that it would point you to being a lawyer, an editor, or a diplomat."

She paused for a moment, "A lawyer," she said.

"Yes, and if that were too boring for you, an editor, or diplomat," I repeated.

She kept twirling and seemed to invite more. So I kept at it, telling her how it was not too early to start thinking about these subjects.

In a minute, she left, showered, and then came back and we watched a half hour of a TV comedy. She sat in a comfortable chair, wearing her night garb, which is always the same, a long T-shirt. Later she headed off to bed. I turned off the light feeling a lot better about Mary.

19

Bill and Hillary's
Excellent Adventure

"*K*ids need new experiences, new people to open their minds to new thoughts. It's so important," a friend who had raised his boisterous stepsons told me.

So a plan began to percolate in my brain, a plan to take us out of the unrelenting heat of Texas across the southern part of the United States into the majesty and intrigue of Washington, D.C., and, ultimately, to the cool breezes of Long Island's Hamptons for a month of sun, sand, and serenity. It would be a summer packed with memories. It would cost. It would really cost. But it was something I wanted to give them, something I wanted them to experience. I wanted the kids to see my Washington, the city I had known and loved so well through nine administrations. I knew I had better do it soon.

On a good day I can get around with the help of a cane; on a bad day I'm really in trouble. One thing I knew for sure was that I wouldn't be able to tolerate the torturous drive across country. So Paula would be in charge of that leg (pun intended). She is a strong and beautiful twenty-seven-year-old with good judgment and steady nerves. In many ways, she is like an overgrown kid who finds happiness everywhere, even in driving teenagers with their blaring rock 'n' roll, cyberpunk, and coffee-shop folk music over fifteen hundred miles from Texas to the nation's capital. She loves politics, pizzas, and presidents. A university graduate, she had a tremendous liking for national politics, an up-to-date knowledge of it, and the warmest smile I have ever seen.

We talked about our trip for weeks. Mary would rather stay home with her friends. No way, I told her. Well, then she wanted to take her green Doc Martens combat boots to walk around in and her entire CD collection to play along the way. I could live with that. Hell, I wasn't going to be in the car. But I did secretly think I might try to lose the boots accidentally in the packing.

Talking about and planning are half the fun of travel. They would take my car with handicapped plates. Until recently, I had always thought there were too many handicapped parking places at the grocery store and the mall. No more! I was fast becoming a lobbyist for the cause. Paula and Tommy would share the driving. They would drive through Louisiana, Mississippi, stop at Memphis to see Graceland, Elvis Presley's home (Paula's idea, because she is a nut about Elvis), then hit the Hermitage in Nashville, home of Andrew Jackson, the Southern populist, on through North Carolina to Asheville to visit Thomas Wolfe's home, up through Virginia to Thomas Jefferson's town, Charlottesville, so Tommy could take a look at the University of Virginia, and then Monticello, and finally into Washington, D.C.! The presidential homes were *my* idea.

I would take a plane and meet them in Washington. My fourteen-year-old grandson, Les, from Seattle, would meet us there. At the last minute Mary decided she would rather fly, too, so it was up to Paula and Tommy and Tommy's good friend, Bianca Toness, to bring the car.

I gave them my parting formula for travel: Go with all the senses in action—including sight, sound, *and* taste. Sample the offerings of regional cooking: Cajun rice and red beans, she-crab soup in Louisiana, catfish in Mississippi, and country ham and biscuits in Tennessee, North Carolina, and Virginia. Breathe in the fragrances of the honeysuckle and magnolia of the South and listen to the sounds of the mighty Mississippi—deep-throated horns on barges filled with men yelling back and forth as they move the big containers of rice and soybeans along toward New Orleans and their final destinations in Asia. I didn't need to alert them to the jazz in Memphis.

With the exception of his trip to Mexico, Tommy's travel had been mostly vicarious through the writings of Jack Kerouac, the Beat generation's spokesman who bummed his way from New Jersey to San Francisco with various friends of questionable character, meeting hoboes and losers, people of every scale. That's not my idea of travel. I prefer Rockefeller accommodations.

It was raining when they left Austin in the early gray drizzle of morning. Tommy was already into his Kerouac mood with his journal and pen in hand. Later Paula reported that when they passed the Texas capitol, Tommy mused aloud about the capitol "shrouded in a cloak of mist." He was already composing before they reached the city limits.

I kept up with their travels by nightly phone calls—and there were lots of them. I was eager to hear the news of this trip I wished I could have taken. I have known and loved the sleepy beauty of the South all my life. I have also despaired of its shortcomings and thrilled to the progress made by a Southern-born president who cajoled and strong-armed civil-rights laws through Congress.

The night when Tommy called to report they were safely in Memphis, he read me a few lines from his journal of the day. "The river rumbled by like I will never return." We talked about how, in a sense, he really wouldn't return, at least not as the boy who drove out of the city limits. I quoted from somewhere in the back of my mind: "No one bathes in the same stream twice, for yesterday's waters have gone on to the sea."

Tommy, Paula, and Bianca continued on from Memphis, forever changed by the visit to Elvis's homesite. His music rocked from the car tape player those last several hundred miles, until they all knew the lyrics to the entire canon. Soon enough we would all know them too, as Elvis became our patron saint and mandatory source of all traveling music.

Finally, at long last, we were all six together in Washington—Tommy, Mary, Bianca, Paula, my grandson Les, and I. There was so much I wanted them to do and know: stories for Tommy and Mary about their father, who introduced me to the city fifty years ago, stories for Les about the grandfather he never knew—my own Les—when he and I were young and racing about the city covering the great moments in history at the Capitol, the Supreme Court, and the White House from FDR to JFK.

When I first came there on that June day in 1942, as World War II was in full throttle, it was my brother

Tom, then working for the Roosevelt administration, who picked me up at the airport. Those were prejet days, and the flight from Austin to Washington took eight hours. Tom swung the car in front of the Lincoln Memorial on our way to his home and we bounded up the steps to stand at the feet of President Lincoln. For me, it will always be the perfect way for newcomers to meet the city. Now the kids bounded up those same steps. I took it a little easier. I was in a rented wheelchair so I didn't lose steam before noon, so Paula took me to the top by elevator.

It was eight in the evening as we stood between the columns of the Lincoln Memorial, and on this summer night twilight was fading into nightfall and the twinkling lights of the city. I lifted my cane and repeated my favorite toast: "To Washington, central star of the constellation, may it enlighten the whole world." It was the adapted toast General Lafayette had given in his ceremonial tour of the United States in 1824. I had discovered it in working on a toast for President Johnson to use with a foreign visitor. What better way to begin our four days than to repeat it in our starting place atop the Lincoln Memorial steps.

My heart was really in this trip. Allen Drury's classic description has always summarized the city for me, and I reconstructed it for them now: "Washington, the great white marbled capital . . . in which evil men do good things and good men do evil in a way of life only Americans can understand and often they are baffled."

It is a town of constant political drama, but also home to families who live through the milestones of personal life surrounded by the overpowering national news and the characters who create it. Here I had married, known motherhood, and experienced grief and widowhood. Thirty-five years I lived here— half of my life.

What did it hold for me, this Washington I fell in love with on my arrival? Beauty, intrigue, in-the-know conversations, the breathless waiting through a tight vote on Capitol Hill, the over-the-shrimp-bowl gossip at five o'clock. If you were young and a reporter, there was no escaping the spell this great city of power and glory offered, this listening post for the world, this revolving door for heads of state, this democracy in which we all hold a sense of personal ownership.

The kids loved reading aloud the words of Lincoln from the walls: "Four score and seven years ago . . ." Most of them knew them from schoolbooks. Here in the shadow of the man, the words came to life. I noticed that Mary was drinking in every word, almost transfixed.

For weeks now, I had been advancing the trip as

though I were escort officer for some visiting poten-
tate, calling up every old friend with entrance to the
temple gates. It was an operation of fax and phone to
contacts at Capitol Hill and the White House, to
friends in the Hamptons, where we would go after the
Washington trip. Everything fell into place miracu-
lously. My old friends rushed to get passes for entrance here and there; my White House contacts said
the presidential box at the Kennedy Center for the
Performing Arts was mine for an evening. I thanked
my lucky stars for Hillary Rodham Clinton, a friend
of many years. A few months before, I had invited her
to come to Austin to deliver a lecture named in my
honor at the University of Texas. It had been a fantastic success. Fourteen thousand cheering students and townspeople filled the biggest auditorium
on the campus. She had spoken forty-five minutes
without a note and wowed everyone with a plea for a
politics of meaning, for redefining ourselves and our
role as citizens. I had the challenge of not only getting
her there, but also introducing her. I did so by saying
she was "America's daughter, my daughter, your
daughter. To me, she is what the women's movement
is all about."

Now, we were in her town with my blue notebook
and detailed schedule—"The Bible," we called it, just
as I had the itineraries of presidents and first ladies

back in the sixties. We were awash with significant phone numbers up and down the Eastern Seaboard, invitations, and special tours of the key buildings.

Fortunately we were bedded down each night at the spacious McLean, Virginia, home of Senator and Mrs. Charles Robb—Chuck and Lynda Johnson Robb—whose wedding I had helped manage back in my White House years. The house literally sits two hundred feet above the shoals of the Potomac River, which rushes along from McLean to Georgetown past National Airport to Mount Vernon, home of the first president.

My bedroom overlooked the Potomac's waters below and became the gathering place each day to powwow about the day's adventures. I inserted any history I knew or uncovered.

"Right here in 1608 Captain John Smith passed along these waters from the Jamestown settlement." At night I would reread Washington guidebooks to bone up on details.

"Were we kin to any Indians?" Mary asked.

"The best," I shot back, "Pocahontas, who married John Rolfe."

Tommy let out a war whoop, but Mary, now moving into adolescent cynicism, just curled her lips and retreated, disbelieving, to her earphones and corn chips.

We also met twice a day to discuss what to wear

and how to behave. Especially after Hillary Rodham Clinton sent word that I was invited to a dinner for sixty at the White House the following evening. "Bring the children," I was advised. "They can have a pizza party with Chelsea in the solarium on the top floor of the White House."

I couldn't wait to get off the phone and tell them, and see their astonished faces. They didn't disappoint me. All day, they had been saying things like "fantastic" and Les's favorite expression, "awesome." Now, what was there left to say except to jump up and down and hug each other excitedly? The Washington tour was unfolding beyond my wildest dreams.

I was a girl again, full of the old memories and history lessons that swept me up when I came here. They began to surface in my mind's eye, like a kaleidoscope of scenes and people and stories back to George Washington's time when he met the surveyors at various pubs in Georgetown. I pointed out the spires of Georgetown and tried to crowd in everything I knew as we talked. Age makes you a history buff because you have, or at least I have, always wanted to know who walked these streets, what ghosts wrote history here. I am not a collector of period furniture or curtain styles in old houses, but of the lives of the people who lived there. That's why before we got to the White House I told the kids about the chilly November day when Abigail Adams arrived by coach, having gotten lost twice coming through the Maryland forests. I told them about all the lower rooms being open in the early day; that Dolley Madison had kept her milk cows in the first-floor room where 150 years later I gave my press briefings. Mary got into the spirit of the city and promptly spoke up with a smile, "You moved from moos to news."

I told them about the White House press room. "Thomas Jefferson had his outhouses right here where the press room is now," I said.

And Les, who is a sometime stand-up comic at school, cracked, "It's still a place of shit." And then, I'm glad to say, he blushed.

The kids had begun to treat me with something approaching deference after Tommy spotted my picture in the first ladies' exhibit at the Smithsonian. It was a shot of me holding up the hands of Rosalyn Carter and Betty Ford, at the ERAmerica Salute to First Ladies, and there we were, allies in the fight for women's rights.

Now they were into the whole Washington scene, learning history from the experts I had known through thirty-four years and pressed into service for two or three hours. The kids took turns wheeling me through the nation's Capitol, where I poured some facts and legends into them. The curator of the Senate, Jim Ketchum, mixed humor from old Washington scandals into it. When he greeted us at the door he explained to the security guards, "This is Nan Britton, I'm Warren G. Harding, and these are all our children." One of the guards looked like he believed it.

It wasn't the same Capitol I had known as a young reporter, pad and pencil in hand, running back and forth across the Capitol Rotunda between House and Senate, weaving among the hundreds of tourists who came to see their seat of government each day. Now it is only selected tourists who are free to see it all. What a lot of security has gone up to protect the building from the people of this country, a building I once moved in and out of with such freedom. Today you are stopped: "Give your name, birthdate, and show a picture identification," the guard humorlessly intones. This, even though our escort was an official of the building. There is something ominous about these intimidating checkpoints in which the citizens of this democracy are examined with suspicion before they enter. I don't see how democracy can survive all the multiplying barriers between the citizen and the official. At the very least, all the security is like cold water on the visitor's enthusiasm.

We entered and began craning our necks as Jim pointed at the treasures of the ceiling, the paintings by the Italian artist Brumidi, who came to America in the early 1800s and recorded with his brush in exquisite precision the flora and fauna of this vast new country for a building to hold the legislative arm of representative government. We paused and passed by busts and portraits of the vice presidents and distinguished senators of the past. Jim pointed to the place in the hall outside the Senate Chamber where some still unidentified crazies had bombed the Capitol and destroyed Henry Clay's statue a dozen years ago. That's when this area had been cut off from the public in general, and eight guards at each Capitol door replaced one.

My favorite word-pictures of the Capitol Building begin with the earliest days, when the rotunda was the marketplace for Washington and vendors sold chickens, pigs, and vegetables there. Nearby, in the old Senate Chamber, we had the giants of the time: John Calhoun, Henry Clay, and Daniel Webster debating the structure and regulations of the burgeoning country.

Sam Houston would sit and carve wooden hearts and send them to ladies in the gallery where the town's social leaders as well as the general public were seated.

It was a time of plenty of time. "Once Senator Daniel Webster was four hours into a speech when Dolley Madison arrived in the gallery and he began it again," Jim recalled.

And then he told us how John Randolph of Virginia

would arrive late with his hunting dogs and muddy boots from tromping through the marshy Tiber River (now Pennsylvania Avenue) and would summon the slave boys from the gallery to bring him a tankard of ale. It was a more freewheeling Senate, even though the practice of "Will the gentleman yield?" existed even then.

We wound up on the House side of the Capitol, where I pointed out Oklahoma's statue of Will Rogers, who had asked that he be placed where he could "keep an eye on Congress." And there he stands, staring at its entrance to the floor of the chamber. As I mentioned, I spared no one in arranging this visit. Old friendships had been rekindled, old contacts rejuvenated shamelessly. Our congressman, Jake Pickle, was given the opportunity to take us to lunch, and he did.

Then we crammed ourselves into the car and headed back to our overnight headquarters at the Robbs' home in Virginia. Their swimming pool was a lifesaver for the kids, weary from the marble floors of government.

The evening built to new excitement. After all, we had the whole presidential box at the Kennedy Center for the Performing Arts. And *Phantom of the Opera* was playing. I decided that since the congressman had picked up the tab at noon we would have dinner in the fancy dining room atop Kennedy Center. I didn't realize how "all out" it would be. We were there by six-thirty, the boys in coats and ties and the rest of us dressed to the nines. I should have checked on the prices! Everything was à la carte: nonalcoholic frozen daiquiris for the kids, ten dollars a shot; entrées at twenty-two dollars and up; and desserts at five dollars for a piece of pie. The waiter kept filibustering the kids to order more—and they didn't mind if they did.

I have noticed that when the kids finally do get all dressed up, they keep the conversation lively and interesting, and tonight was a shining example. All around the dinner table everyone was animated and excited. Not a sullen face to be found. I placed Tommy at the head of the table and he immediately assumed the role of host, offering a toast in the manner of Lafayette.

"To good food and good women," he said with a grand flourish.

But I hadn't foreseen what was coming—the check. It read like the national debt. I kept re-adding it, but there it was: $375 before tip, about $50 for each person (except for Tommy, who ate $78.59 worth, a fact we wouldn't let him forget).

Along with the tickets for the presidential box, handsome in red velour, the White House had sent along the key to the mini-refrigerator that sits in the small parlor outside the box. It got fully explored even before the curtain went up. Fortunately it had Diet Pepsis and ginger ales to be poured into champagne glasses, adding to the glamour of the evening. When the theater darkened, off came Tommy's and Les's unaccustomed coats. *Phantom* was a spectacular show to see in this setting, with all the theatrics of moving sets, giant chandeliers flying out over the orchestra and the audience, rising mists from a lake onstage, and dreamlike boats moving silently over it. The kids were spellbound with the Andrew Lloyd Webber dramatic production. Then, at intermission, we all took advantage of the president's private bathroom for the singular experience of "peeing in the president's pot," as Tommy put it.

Paula was essential to this whole operation, which we had labeled "The Bobbsey Kids Go to Washington." My first introduction to our nation's capital was at age nine when someone gave me *The Bobbsey Twins Go to Washington,* though it was years before I actually got there. And now, the frosting on the cake—an adventure in my new life. Paula and I were a good combination: I had the contacts, the penchant for planning ahead every detail, and the storehouse of stories from fifty years on the political front. Paula had the technique and energy to make it work. I had the ability to tell the kids how to meet presidents: "No dead-fish handshakes. Use a firm hand and a smile and have something interesting or at least polite to say." Paula had the power to make them do it. We were like an intensive course of an Emily Post Finishing School for Teenagers.

So by the time Hillary Clinton had the social secretary call to invite us, as well as Jennifer Robb, to the White House, these kids were picking out their own outfits instead of being forced into them, and their behavior would have been approved by Martha Washington, *Good Housekeeping,* and Miss Manners.

We came, and as far as I could tell, we conquered. Mrs. Clinton greeted us at the diplomatic entrance with warm hugs and introductions. "Come on in," she said. "Chelsea is looking forward to your visit." As I watched her talk and listen to my brood, I realized this is a first lady who *really* understands teenagers.

I enjoyed cocktails in the diplomatic room of the White House and then was escorted by elevator to the second-floor living quarters to visit with the fifty-nine other guests. We were given a private tour of the Lincoln Bedroom and the president's newly created study (formerly the Treaty Room) and then escorted down to the beautiful Blue Room, where six tables of ten were awaiting us.

The kids were taken to the solarium on the third floor to be greeted by Chelsea. Three great-great-grandchildren of Franklin and Eleanor Roosevelt were there, as were two children of the Arkansan movie star, Mary Steenburgen. ("We were served pizza on White House china," Les reported later with the awe of one who has known pizza mostly on paper plates.) Then Chelsea offered her guests a special tour of the entire White House.

"That would be great," Tommy said, rising, and adding, "Why not play hide and seek?" But everyone followed Chelsea to her father's Oval Office, and then to the Cabinet Room, where the kids sat in the chairs of Secretary of Housing Henry Cisneros and Secretary of the Treasury Lloyd Bentsen, our two Texans in the Clinton cabinet, as well as the chairs of the president and vice president. Then onto the pastry kitchen, which impressed Mary even more.

By ten-thirty our dinner for sixty "new friends and old," as President Clinton called us, was over. The first lady sent for Chelsea and the kids in the solarium to come and meet the other guests. I held my breath as I watched Les, Mary, Bianca, Jennifer, and Tommy move toward the president. He turned to them and sure enough, hooray, there were smiles, strong firm handshakes, and an exchange of something I hoped was okay. I wish that I had been closer, to hear the conversation. I heard Tommy say something about Graceland, and the president responded with a laugh. The rest of the crew put their hands over their hearts and I knew they were about to launch into one of the many Elvis songs. Paula must have sensed it too, because she stepped up and guided them on to greet Vice President and Mrs. Gore. After a half hour of mixing, we said farewell to the Clintons, then went back to the Robbs' home. But the kids weren't ready for the pool that night. They had to have an hour to talk about the evening and go over every nuance and detail. By now it was "Bill and Hillary and Al and Tipper, and the funny Senator Simpson, who was in the movie *Dave*, who told us he was the lone Republican present."

Everyone agreed that Chelsea had it tough. "She can't be a kid," Tommy said indignantly. "She must get really tired of having to be nice to people like us."

Mary said sympathetically, "It must be awful to have everyone looking at you all the time and giving opinions on your hairdo." But they gave her an "A plus" for handling it well.

"Would you like to be president?" I posed the question to the group.

"Welllll, maybe."

All in all it was a marvelous summer for me and the children. For each of us, it was a different experience. For Tommy, it was an awakening. For Les, it was a bonding. And for Mary, it was a coming-out party.

It drew us closer as a family. Tommy and Mary

learned how to meet people and sometimes draw them out with questions. At Tommy's insistence, I read Jack Kerouac's *On the Road*. I missed it the first time around, when I was in my thirties and thought I was conversant with the arts of my time. Reading it now, I realized just how much I had missed. And how much I owed this young sturdy boy-man in whom the blood of my ancestors flowed, who slowly was broadening my appreciation of life and its new and unexpected joys just as I hope I was broadening his. My attention span for his music even lengthened from five to ten minutes.

The magical summer filled with presidential hand-shakes, good conversation, and Elvis music lingers on like a hovering cloud of dreams.

20

Reflections

On Sunday mornings the house is quiet until noon, and it is the time my best thoughts come. I have a special Sunday routine, to grind my favorite coffee beans—Viennese with cinnamon—and indulge in a cup of coffee with warm whole milk instead of skimmed. I sit and savor the cup and the day in my office, which is glass on all sides and protrudes from the rest of the house with a spectacular view of the Colorado River and the skyline of the city. From here I watch the theater of the sky. A December sunrise at daybreak is worth total attention. The first rays—vivid scarlet, moving softly into pinks and blues and lavenders—spread out upon the great canvas in the most pleasing manner. Below, the mist rests gently on the river. But only for a minute or two, and then the deep pink and orange of the sun move from the horizon steadily up, spreading their vibrant colors until the sky glows so brightly that it dims the silhouette of the cityscape and the mists lift, revealing the winding river.

With the glare now full blown, I turn from the scene to read the *Daily Word*'s message for the day. Today it was as if God had handed me exactly what I needed. The lesson was on children, and it read:

> Have you ever tried to teach a child something only to discover that you learned far more from the experience than the child did? Through an enthusiasm for learning and growth, the child opened your eyes to a different perspective and taught you the true joy in living.
>
> Children are wonderful expressions of God's love, and they show us how to live life *now*. They teach us to love one another unconditionally, to trust without doubt, to forgive without hesitation, to enjoy life without concern for the future.
>
> By following their example we, too, can live as God meant us to: faith-filled, free, and full of the joy of living.

This was a lesson, not just for today but for life. These children have inspired me, without my even realizing it. They have made me examine carefully the first of life and the last. They have forced me to think about their world and mine, and to realize much is to be gained for young and old by walking hand in hand through the imperfect places along life's route.

I think of the words of Ulysses as he gathered his friends: " 'Tis not too late to seek a newer world. Cast off and, sitting well in order, smite the sounding furrows."

Perhaps we, too—the old and the young of the nineties—can seek a newer world, free of fear, by being here for each other.

So where are we all now . . . three years into each other's lives? They are growing so fast, shooting up almost visibly. Tommy is over six feet tall. I have come to like his shoulder-length hair that frames his personality of rigid idealist. Mary is five feet eight inches, with slender long legs. She is currently a blonde and I hope she will never dye it again as she did once—auburn red. We have all aged. Mary is fifteen and a freshman in high school, popular, strong-willed at times, "like a Sutherland," my brother George reminds me. Tommy is seventeen, a senior in high school with a wide circle of friends. He is easygoing and has his father's capacity for happiness. Liz is nineteen, off at the School of Visual Arts in New York City, working part-time at a video store and torn between a steady boyfriend and homesickness. She misses Tommy and Mary and calls for long telephone conversations.

I believe, and I hope they do, that they will help work their way through college. They grew up with the idea that education is essential and college is assumed. I often quote the slogan "Learning never ends." They are beginning to know, however belatedly, that certain actions do lead to certain consequences. If you fail to do homework, you get caught. If you speed in the car, you get arrested and your insurance goes up. If you do drugs, you don't realize your potential. Here at my house they get a feeling of rules and structure, and a sense that "making something of themselves" is expected of them. I don't believe they will fail.

I asked each of them a three-part question: What kind of college, career, and spouse (if any) do you want for yourself? I did this because I want them to help me summarize where they are in their thinking now.

Liz hasn't wavered from wanting to make a career of working in photography and film, she says, because she likes "the visual way of telling powerful stories with powerful scenes, and lighting and colors that add to the power." Maybe all those vivid Stephen King horror stories led her there.

As for marriage and children, her answer is, "Yes, but in about ten years, and I want someone to share life with who is smart, nice, and funny, who is ambitious and knows where he wants to go."

Tommy, who is facing SAT scores, wants a liberal arts college that has "a certain diligence. But I don't want it to be a cage. I don't want to be in a room making notes with fifty other students. I'm very concerned with the kind of professors I have. I will probably major in philosophy or psychology and roam around before I enter graduate school."

I liked his dreams but wondered how we would finance this indulgence. That hasn't yet entered his conversation or his thinking. Obviously it's something I never stop thinking about.

"You know," he says, "I could never have a job that made me put on a suit and shirt every day and go work in a building like a shut-in."

Marriage? Yes, of course, he wants to marry sometime. "I want to marry someone like Zelda, who was a crazy genius, someone who has the kindness of the womanly attributes, but who has wit and a streak of wildness and who is up for adventure."

Mary is still sorting it all out. Intrigued by the psychic, she, too, called on our town's favorite mystic, who reads your life, past and future, with tarot cards. At Paula's suggestion, Mary carried a notebook and made notes like a professional. She nearly fainted when the psychic turned up a four and a six from the tarot cards, and from that deducted that October 10 was Mary's birthday, which it is. The psychic also told her that she would meet her "real love" when she was twenty-seven at college. He would be very conservative and from an outstanding family. I wondered why it was going to take her to twenty-seven to get to college. Would she be living with me until then? Ye gads!

"The only thing I learned about my career," Mary continued, "is that I will be working with a lot of people."

What are her own thoughts about my question about college, marriage, and career?

She dropped her jaw, "I don't have any idea."

Maybe the best clue lies in a poem that Mary wrote in the seventh grade. One of her teachers sent it to me. I had never suspected that she was quite so gifted at unveiling her feelings.

> Love, life, and literature
> Within themselves I find myself,
> With the love I want to live
> With the life I can love
> Literature finds itself within me
> I will know it when I find myself.
> —Mary Sutherland

As for Nancy, their mother, she seems pleased with the situation. "It was wrenching for them to have to move from the house where they were living," she tells me. "But they were familiar with you and your house all their lives. Their growth has been phenomenal, physically and mentally. Feeling happy and being in a happy place, having a good diet and the help of a caring aunt who shows an interest in their projects has meant everything. It has also freed me to train for and find a job."

As for me, it came as an awful shock to find that I am the same age as the pope. That turned up in the news when he fell and broke his shoulder recently.

Now I am seventy-four, subject to all the lapses of energy that seventy-four-year-old people are, but hooray, hooray, the hobbling foot is free of pain and I move about better now than I did last year before the ankle fusion. I am still earning the major living for all of us by writing and speaking and am grateful to God, the publishers, and lecture agent that I have a steady market. I enjoy doing that and can't imagine giving up either the activity or the income, whether I am earning it for all of us or just me. I've visited enough nursing homes to know I don't want to be there and settle into God's waiting room. Save me from that! Maybe these kids have.

I truly love them and I miss them when they are not here. I worry about them, probably too much. I have high hopes for them, which I tell them about whenever they aren't off doing their own thing and will listen.

But I can still be heartbreakingly disappointed and angry when they fail to do homework and depressed at their constant habit of trashing up their rooms, and of walking around lost in their own worlds.

I still ask myself: Is this typical of teenagers? My friends answer yes and begin their tales of woe.

I can also be terribly proud of each one at different times, and I find them increasingly interesting human beings and good conversationalists. I like them as young people, know their strengths and shortcomings, and I have faith that they will make it somehow.

Would I recommend what I have done to anyone else? To borrow their phrase, "Not really." Not if there is anyone younger and more agile who will take it on. I had only two qualifications: I was willing and I had done it before. But if it is a matter of you doing it or no one will, you must.

In today's world, no one should have children who is not willing to make them a major constant in their lives. It takes tremendous energy and hard work to guide them through the teenage years unharmed.

"Mine is the orphan generation," Tommy mused. "I have only two friends who live with both their natural parents. For the rest it is one or three."

"What effect do you think that will have on your generation?" I asked.

He paused, thought, and finally said, "We'll either be as worthless as the lowest dogs, or we will seek love supreme."

My time with these children has brought out the preacher in me. We—every adult, even those without children—need to be on the alert to furnish a lifeline to the child who comes your way. It may be as simple as a compliment, or as easy as a treat to the movies, or, better still, an offer to help them study. It may merely be looking into their eyes and listening to them. A lot is at stake—a whole generation, maybe two, of children who are neglected or unbonded to an adult. How many can our society absorb who are lost to ignorance, to drugs, to crime? Our streets, our happiness, our country are all in peril if we leave the children of our frightening times to chance.

Am I glad I did it? Emphatically yes. Not because it was a barrel of fun. Not because they are so grateful, which they aren't. But because, as I said, I would rather do it than fail to do it.

It has tested me in the winter of my life, and it has reassured me that I am strong enough to meet what life hands me. In some ways, it has been more challenging than the experiences of my past life, however vigorous and invigorating they were, because it has extracted more from me. Those experiences of sipping champagne by moonlight at the Acropolis, of dancing in the East Room of the White House, of riding a whistlestop train through Dixie with a president, were great fun for the moment, but ultimately they were not lasting, they weren't as demanding, well, really, as difficult as this has been.

Next to raising my own children, taking on these three young people may be one of the most important things I have ever done, and I pray it works. Certainly it has widened my world and served me a slice of my country's future I would not have otherwise known. I have learned firsthand how tough the world is for kids and for those who love them.

Of course, I don't know the ending of their story and probably never will. I will die or they will move on before it's revealed how Liz, Tommy, and Mary turn out. But that's the risk of uncertainty that life imposes on all its great challenges.

About the Author

At seventy-four, LIZ CARPENTER is still at it: writing books and articles and riding the lecture circuit from her home, Grass Roots, in the hills overlooking Austin, Texas.

Walter Cronkite says: "Liz Carpenter is much more than an American original: she is an American and a Texas original. Her inside stories of our nation's political life over the last half-century are priceless."

A descendant of five generations of Texans, Liz Carpenter went to Washington at age twenty-two to cover the White House of Franklin and Eleanor Roosevelt. In 1960, she moved from her reportorial beat to work with her fellow Texans Lyndon and Lady Bird Johnson. During this past year her friendship with Bill and Hillary Clinton brought her back for a White House visit, this time with the teenagers she had inherited from her late brother.

The author is a Distinguished Alumna of the University of Texas, a member of the Texas Women's Hall of Fame, a director of the National Wildflower Research Center, and a recipient of numerous awards and honorary degrees. She was a founder of the National Women's Political Caucus and an activist for the Equal Rights Amendment.

About the Type

This book was set in Bookman, which was the name given to the original typeface Old Style Antique by Wadsworth A. Parker at the turn of the century. The first cutting of Old Style Antique was made in 1858 by Miller & Richard, a Scottish foundry, and occurred because of the need for a typeface with greater weight than the standard old-style faces possessed.